MAJOR EUROPEAN AUTHORS

TWO FRENCH MORALISTS
La Rochefoucauld and La Bruyère

TWO FRENCH MORALISTS
La Rochefoucauld &
La Bruyère

ODETTE DE MOURGUES

Fellow of Girton College and Professor of French in
the University of Cambridge

CAMBRIDGE UNIVERSITY PRESS
CAMBRIDGE
LONDON · NEW YORK · MELBOURNE

Published by the Syndics of the Cambridge University Press
The Pitt Building, Trumpington Street, Cambridge CB2 1RP
Bentley House, 200 Euston Road, London NW1 2DB
32 East 57th Street, New York, NY 10022, USA
296 Beaconsfield Parade, Middle Park, Melbourne 3206, Australia

First published 1978

Printed in Great Britain
at the University Press, Cambridge

Library of Congress Cataloguing in Publication Data
Mourgues, Odette de.
Two French moralists
(Major European authors)
Bibliography: p.
Includes index.
1. La Rochefoucauld, François, duc de, 1613–1680 –
Criticism and interpretation. 2. La Bruyère, Jean de,
1645–1696 – Criticism and interpretation. I. Title.
PQ1815.M68   848'.4   77-82506
ISBN 0 521 21823 3

GENERAL PREFACE TO THE SERIES

The *Major European Authors* series, as the name implies, considers the most important writers of the European literatures, most often giving a volume to each author, but occasionally treating a group or a genre. The basic assumption is that the general reader and the student will be able to find information on biography and literary history fairly easily elsewhere. What he will look for in this series is a single volume which gives a critical survey of the entire oeuvre or the most important works. Authors of books in the series are asked to keep this general objective in mind: to write critical introductions which will help the reader to order his impressions of the works of art themselves; to assume little prior knowledge, and so far as possible either to quote in English or to translate quotations.

It is hoped that the series will help to keep the classics of European literature alive and active in the minds of present-day readers: both those reading for a formal literary examination, and those who in the original langages and in translation wish to keep in touch with the culture of Europe.

To the memory of
my father
who was for me
a living example
of the moralist's lucidity
courage and human sympathy

CONTENTS

FOREWORD

The scope of this study is limited. It does not attempt to examine with equal thoroughness all the aspects of the two moralists' works, but deals with certain features in their writings; those which for a long time have attracted my curiosity. Nor do I claim to have successfully clarified what, either in the *Maximes* or the *Caractères*, are for me tantalising problems.

Some other critics whose names will appear in the following chapters have during the past ten or twenty years considered the two writers in the same spirit, trying to bring new light to bear on books which have been for too long safely enclosed in well-acknowledged theories about seventeenth-century literature, and thought to be within range of the school curriculum, even if unlikely to provoke much enthusiasm.

I am moved by a similar, if not stronger, urge to question a number of accepted views and to break the respectable but rigid mould which, in its appointed place in the Pantheon of French writers, encases the once living text. My hope is not so much to win the reader over to my own interpretations as to convince him that he should pursue the quest.

ODETTE DE MOURGUES

CAMBRIDGE
March 1977

A NOTE ON SOURCES

Unless otherwise stated, the editions of the two moralists' works used in this book are:

La Rochefoucauld: *Maximes suivies des Réflexions diverses, du Portrait de La Rochefoucauld par lui-même et des Remarques de Christine de Suède sur les Maximes.* Texte établi par Jacques Truchet, Paris, Garnier, 1967

La Bruyère: *Les Caractères de Théophraste traduits du grec avec Les Caractères ou les Moeurs de ce siècle.* Texte établi par Robert Garapon, Paris, Garnier, 1962.

Abbreviations:

M.P. refers to Maximes Posthumes
M.S. refers to Maximes Supprimées

LA ROCHEFOUCAULD

I

TENTATIVE APPROACHES

There is no simple approach to the *Maximes*. Everyone studying the work is tempted to suspect previous criticism of having chosen the wrong angle. It may be, as was convincingly stated in a recent book on La Rochefoucauld, that, whatever the amount of scholarship devoted to the elucidation of his writings, we still lack the evidence which would enable us to read them with full understanding.[1] It is probably a good thing that we should go on circling round the work trying in different ways to get nearer to a clear and accurate appreciation of La Rochefoucauld's thought and art. But it is very possible that all the converging efforts to illuminate the text will inevitably leave it with some blurred outlines and a few inscrutable features.

The architectural pattern of the *Maximes* escapes us. We cannot even guess what it might have been. La Rochefoucauld in different 'Avis au Lecteur' apologised for an absence of method and logical order in the grouping of the maxims but did little to remedy the apparent disorder of the work. Now and then we find a succession of several maxims bearing on the same subject, as a sign perhaps of a coalescing process which remained too fragmentary even to suggest the possibility of a homogeneous whole. Comparisons between the successive editions of the work, critical commentaries on the link between the *Maximes* and the *Réflexions Diverses*, have thrown some interesting light on La Rochefoucauld's creative technique and on a certain evolution in the scope of his work.[2] But in fact we tend to read La Rochefoucauld's writings en bloc. Their very fragmentation allows us to group the *Maximes*

---

[1] See W. G. Moore's Introduction to his book *La Rochefoucauld, his Mind and Art*, Oxford, 1969.

[2] Among the scholars who have been concerned with the genesis of the *Maximes* I can mention here only J. Truchet in his introduction to his edition of the *Maximes*, W. G. Moore in chapters 2 and 3 of his book (op. cit.) and Amelia Bruzzi (*La Formazione delle 'Maximes' di La Rochefoucauld attraverso le edizioni originali*, Bologna, Pàtron, 1968).

Supprimées and the *Maximes Posthumes* round the main bulk of the maxims contained in the 1668 edition and to complete the architectural ensemble by the *Réflexions Diverses* in the same way as we preserve the artificial unity of a building while flanking it with two wings and adding a few larger rooms at the back, over the buried traces of former constructions; with the *Maximes* the substructure being of course constituted by the chronological strata provided by the variants of the first editions.[1] Within this convenient arrangement we have to accept a state of disorder which was perhaps intended, can be partially accounted for and even justified. We shall not find a systematic study of man in La Rochefoucauld.

But he gives us a study of man, and the word moralist may help us as a starting-point. If we take the word with its French connotation, it should at least limit the sphere of La Rochefoucauld's comments on the human condition. The French moralist studies man within the world of nature and reason in a non-metaphysical, non-religious way. Moreover he is not a *moralisateur* and has no system of ethics to propound. He is content to examine man's behaviour (including man's moral attitudes) as it is, with some kind of clear-sighted objectivity. To view the *Maximes* as the work of a *moraliste* appears a sensible assumption. It also fits in with some general features of French classicism, with the tidy, if oversimplified, picture we have of a 'two-truth world' in which religion and philosophy were left to the specialists like Pascal or Bossuet while the purely literary works – Molière's comedies, Racine's tragedies, La Fontaine's *Fables, La Princesse de Clèves* – were focussed on what man can know of himself and of society without any supernatural explanation. There is certainly an affinity between La Rochefoucauld and La Fontaine: the latter praised the *Maximes* for being a faithful mirror of man's true features.[2] Admittedly, in a number of maxims La Rochefoucauld refers specifically to God, but all the critics who have

---

[1] Dominique Secretan's edition of La Rochefoucauld (*Réflexions ou Sentences et Maximes Morales, Réflexions Diverses*, T.L.F., Genève, Paris, 1967), which gives the variants of previous editions under each maxim, adopts a pattern which corresponds very well to this 'architectural' reconstruction.

[2] 'L'homme et son image', *Fables*, I, xi.

commented on the changes made from one edition to another have noted that he removed those maxims as if he was aiming at a *laïcisation* of his picture of man.

Was the *laïcisation* altogether possible? For some readers and commentators the *Maximes* should be read against a background of philosophical influences (Epicureanism for instance) or religious preoccupations (Augustinianism and Jansenism). We are thus led towards a slightly different meaning of the term moralist which is no longer incompatible with ethico-religious concerns, something much nearer to the meaning of the English word, the elasticity of which entitles one to speak of 'Christian moralists' without being guilty of using a self-contradictory expression. It is with this meaning in mind that A. Levi wrote his illuminating study of the French Moralists,[1] and included La Rochefoucauld in the chapter 'The need for grace', side by side with Pascal. Even if, like myself, one would not consider La Rochefoucauld a Christian moralist, it might be rash to dismiss altogether the religious background to the *Maximes*; it may prove relevant to some of the difficulties we shall meet in the elucidation of the work.

From theology to drawing-room pastimes, from the eminently serious to the pleasantly frivolous: why not begin in those salons where the first maxims were formulated? The exchange of letters between Madame de Sablé and La Rochefoucauld discussing the maxims is just one step removed from the conversations in the salon. We conjure up the atmosphere of witty exchanges of epigrams between friends belonging to the same intimate set of sophisticated men and women, the pleasurable competition in finding the brilliant formula, the unexpected paradox, as a conclusion or a starting-point to a debate on a general topic. Discussing fine shades of feeling, points of morals or behaviour was a long-established tradition in the salons, going back to the first *précieuses*. Here the limitations to the scope of the maxims would be firmly set by the requirements of polite society, whose very existence rests on conventions. How far can criticism of the human condition

---

[1] *French Moralists*, Oxford, 1964.

go when the golden rule is not to upset, where the dose of reality, of truth, must be tactfully calculated? If we overstress the link between the *Maximes* and the salon will it not be tantamount to considering them as drawing-room entertainment and a warning not to take them too seriously? In fact to a number of readers they have appeared little more than a clever literary exercise. On the other hand that assessment is no longer tenable as soon as one realises the depth of probing implied in some of the maxims and the upsetting nature of the work. We know that the author's friends were made uneasy, were even shocked. It seems obvious that La Rochefoucauld's investigations had taken him into the kind of austere country where the searching mind is necessarily and painfully alone.

We should not, however, go too far in minimising the importance of social life. No one can fail to notice that a number of maxims or *réflexions* deal specifically with questions of social behaviour, (for instance, with what makes a man agreeable or boring in polite circles) or overlook the long sections in the *Réflexions Diverses*, 'De la société', 'De l'air et des manières', 'De la conversation'. Besides, if we stop thinking of the salon as a procrustean bed imposing its limitations on the creative process of a writer, we realise that there is no incompatibility between the artificial, often frivolous, at times silly, *vie de salon* and a serious interest in human problems. Does the quality of experience depend on the milieu where it collects its material? We may even wonder, when reading Proust and spending so many hours in the Verdurin salon or at parties in the *hôtel de Guermantes*, whether social life is not, for the right kind of observer, the best way of perceiving the ambiguity of human relations, the discrepancies between cause and effect and the subjectivity of one's personal reactions. Nowhere else, perhaps, can the discerning mind so clearly distinguish the many layers hidden beneath the utterance of a value-judgement or beneath the unquestioned respect for a convention. This multiplicity of layers is reflected in the *Maximes* and constitutes one more difficulty in our understanding of the work. We easily notice the element of verticality, the movement which goes from the superficial appearance to what lies underneath. But not all the maxims seize human experience at the same depth. For instance, all the observations concerning women remain very near the surface, at the level of what was traditionally and socially expected or not expected from the female sex, probably because there introspection was impossible. Certain concepts, the idea of *honnêteté* among others, are sometimes examined in connexion with manners, but also in other maxims with reference to the deeper strata of our moral self. These variations in the level of experience chosen for each maxim may to a certain extent account for the impression of fragmentation or the apparent contradictions to be found in the work.

The difficulties I have so far mentioned are closely related to what is perhaps the central obstacle to a satisfactory approach to the *Maximes*: the elusive meaning of some of the words. Not that we lack methodical studies of La Rochefoucauld's style. Vocabulary, grammar, even spelling have been carefully examined. The excellent modern editions we possess have glossaries or abundant footnotes and warn us whenever the connotation of a word has altered since the seventeenth century.

Moreover, according to the scholars who have commented on La Rochefoucauld's diction, we should expect him to have used *le mot juste*. 'Quant à la justesse des mots, au goût sévère, au rapport avec l'idée...il [La Rochefoucauld] demeure un modèle achevé.'[1] This judgement of Henri Regnier, who devoted so much time and patience to a *Lexique de la langue de La Rochefoucauld*, is echoed with even stronger emphasis in a more recent work on the style of the *Maximes*.[2] I am not altogether happy about the expression 'le mot juste' especially when it suggests, as in the above quotation, the complete and

---

[1] *Lexique de la langue de La Rochefoucauld*, avec une introduction grammaticale, in *Oeuvres de La Rochefoucauld*, 'Collection des Grands Ecrivains de France', Tome III, Part II, p. iv, ed. D. L. Gilbert, J. Gourdault, A. et H. Regnier, Paris, 1888–93.
[2] Sister M. F. Zeller, *New Aspects of Style in the Maxims of La Rochefoucauld*, Washington, D.C., Catholic University of America Press, 1954.

unambiguous identity between word and idea. One may also suspect that some of the qualities ascribed to the style of the *Maximes*, in the way they are formulated, derive from a number of assumptions concerning French classicism which might well be questioned.

We have often been told that the evolution of the language and of its cultural background during the seventeenth century provided the classicists with a fitting tool for the creation of literary masterpieces. I wonder. The problem is too large to be properly considered here,[1] but one might venture to say that the greatest achievement of the French classicists was their successful struggle with a language which was in itself very inadequate for their purpose, and that we owe masterpieces to what was in fact a linguistic crisis and, more particularly, a constant battle against the 'je ne sais quoi'. The neutrality and transparency of the language, the dangerous expansion of possible meanings in an abstract noun, the devaluation in the evocative power of imagery set difficult problems for the writer. We know how La Fontaine could overcome the almost impossible task of writing poetry only by elaborating a subtle network of words taken from different traditions and reacting upon one another so as to create in the *Fables* exquisite variations in the semantic field. Another solution was to take the neutrality of the language as the very basis of a literary technique. Few words would be necessary, as their connotation, their intellectual and affective value would depend entirely on the context. Racinian tragedy presents the tightest possible contextual fabric, and the interdependence of its various elements gives to the most inert or imprecise term effective sharpness and explosive power. A great orator like Bossuet could take advantage of the vagueness in the import of a word and paradoxically create the strongest emotive effect

---

[1] A certain evolution of language from the sixteenth to the seventeenth century has been analysed by Michel Foucault in *Les Mots et les Choses*, N.R.F., 1966. His comments are remarkable and fascinating, but I am not sure that they help us very much with the problem of language as a literary tool. For a different opinion see J. Culler's article: 'Paradox and the language of morals in La Rochefoucauld' in *Modern Language Review*, January, 1973, pp. 28–39, in which he bases most of his interesting analyses on Foucault.

out of the very impotence of the language, when referring to the decaying state of our body after death as 'un je ne sais quoi qui n'a plus de nom dans aucune langue'. In a different way the flexibility of the vocabulary could be used for dialectical purposes and allow Pascal to write his famous aphorism – for some a strikingly convincing conceit and for others a specious play on words – 'le coeur a ses raisons que la raison ne connaît point'.

What of La Rochefoucauld? In a way one might think that the characteristics of the seventeenth-century language were well suited to the literary form he had chosen, if we admit that the success of a maxim rests on the wide range of meaning within the narrow limits of a brief sentence. In that case the expanding power of connotation latent in word might be turned to advantage in increasing the wealth of suggestions created by the maxim.

On the other hand the greater part of the *Maximes* is concerned with psychological investigations which require fine distinctions and therefore an accurate and sensitive instrument. It is irrelevant, of course, to think of the technical terminology which our scientific modern age has at its disposal when it studies the working of the human mind. But we may think of Montaigne. For him only the concrete language could seize the ever moving, ever changing, multicoloured quality of our psychological life. As for the traditional abstract terms expressing the activities of the mind, he could afford to treat them with a certain amount of *désinvolture*: they were just the more fluid elements in the rich context of his explorations.

The amount of concrete language La Rochefoucauld can use is limited to a few conventional images. The problem he faces is the same as the difficulties met by the other classicists but in a much more acute form. Here again, as in Racine, the value of the word, its exact shade of meaning, will depend on the context; but the context given by a single maxim is at times practically non-existent. Should the context be provided by the *Maximes* taken as a whole? Only up to a point if we think of the fragmentation of the work and of the different levels of

experience La Rochefoucauld is concerned with. What is
more, given the subject of his investigation, some words may
not be conveniently neutral and docile. The analysis of man's
thoughts, feelings and behaviour had been, particularly in his
century, closely linked with questions of Christian dogma or
Christian ethics. A word such as 'amour-propre', for instance,
will be loaded with theological implications or *a priori*
value-judgements.

It is sometimes relatively easy for the reader to distinguish
between different connotations given to the same word in
different contexts. Let us take for example the term *honnêteté*
which I mentioned previously.

Les faux honnêtes gens sont ceux qui déguisent leurs défauts aux
autres et à eux-mêmes. Les vrais honnêtes gens sont ceux qui les
connaissent parfaitement et les confessent. (202)

Le vrai honnête homme est celui qui ne se pique de rien. (203)

The foot-note by J. Truchet comments, quite rightly I think,
that *honnête* in the first maxim has a moral connotation, but
in the second refers to the social ideal of the *honnête homme.*

At another level of experience, that concerning women
(who, as I have already said, constitute a special category
of human beings), the word *honnêteté* assumes a different
meaning corresponding to a moral code which applied only
to women:

L'honnêteté des femmes est souvent l'amour de leur réputation et
de leur repos. (205)

We scarcely need the variants from previous editions to guess
that here *honnêteté* means chastity.

Conversely, the context of the maxim and the coupling of
two maxims may enable us to perceive and accept a difference
of meaning between two words which we might have considered as interchangeable in the seventeenth century.

La politesse de l'esprit consiste à penser des choses honnêtes et
délicates. (99)

La galanterie de l'esprit est de dire des choses flatteuses d'une manière
agréable. (100)

The distinction is clear on the whole although we may be side-tracked by the ambiguity of *honnêtes* in maxim 99. If we take it with its moral connotation the distance between *politesse* and *galanterie* will obviously be greater than if it refers to a morally indifferent quality of the civilised man, a sort of intellectual elegance which colours his unspoken thoughts.

This wish to establish graded differences between words belonging to related vocabulary appears several times in the *Maximes*. But the distinctions are not always clear, or seem to be contradicted by other maxims. J. Truchet notes that the opposition between *esprit* and *jugement* stated firmly in two maxims:

Le bon goût vient plus du jugement que de l'esprit. (258)

On est quelquefois un sot avec de l'esprit, mais on ne l'est jamais avec du jugement. (456)

clashes with maxim 97 in which La Rochefoucauld affirms the identity of judgement with *esprit* (On s'est trompé lorsqu'on a cru que l'esprit et le jugement étaient deux choses différentes. Le jugement n'est que la grandeur de la lumière de l'esprit...).[1]

La Rochefoucauld's contemporaries found the *Maximes* somewhat obscure at times. And modern scholars and critics confess that they do not find all of them perfectly intelligible, although it is worth noting that they are not all puzzled by the same maxims.

To what extent would a comparison with the vocabulary of other writers in the century prove a help? It is difficult to say. The word *finesse* in Pascal is a word of praise, but it has a pejorative connotation in La Rochefoucauld, for whom it signifies a rather low form of cunning (as opposed to *habileté*). On the other hand W. G. Moore is tempted to think that La Rochefoucauld's use of the word *cœur* might be very near the Pascalian implication of 'unconscious decision' (as opposed to *esprit* which is conscious thinking) in some maxims such as

[1] See p. 66, footnote 3.

11

L'esprit est toujours la dupe du cœur. (102)

Tous ceux qui connaissent leur esprit ne connaissent pas leur cœur. (103)[1]

It is an interesting suggestion, but I still consider (perhaps wrongly) *cœur* to mean sensibility in these maxims. The more one reads the *Maximes* the more one realises how much one has taken for granted, and one starts questioning previous interpretations. Even words which seemed so ordinary as to be innocent of any ambiguity may prove recalcitrant on re-reading.

I am particularly interested in La Rochefoucauld's use of the word *force*, and will come back to it later in this study. It is perhaps this element of fascination, even if it may lead us astray, which adds extra dimensions to our reading of the book.

La Rochefoucauld certainly realised the frustrating inadequacy of language when it comes to shades of meaning and to the faithful rendering of what we intend to express. There is a very revealing passage in one of the *Réflexions Diverses*. After commenting on the different ways in which one can qualify *l'esprit*: 'esprit utile' and 'esprit d'affaires', 'esprit fin' and 'esprit de finesse', 'bel esprit' etc., he finds these qualifying epithets far from satisfactory, as may be seen in the following extract:

Bien qu'il y ait plusieurs épithètes pour l'esprit qui paraissent une même chose, le ton et la manière de les prononcer y mettent de la différence: mais comme les tons et les manières ne se peuvent écrire, je n'entrerai point dans un détail qu'il serait impossible de bien expliquer. L'usage ordinaire le fait assez entendre, et en disant qu'un homme a de l'esprit, qu'il a bien de l'esprit, qu'il a beaucoup d'esprit, et qu'il a bon esprit, il n'y a que le ton et les manières qui puissent mettre de la différence entre ces expressions qui paraissent semblables sur le papier, et qui expriment néanmoins de très différentes sortes d'esprit.

(XVI – De la différence des esprits)

[1] Op. cit., p. 62.

The whole *Réflexion* is concerned with definitions and classification yet states the fallacy of the classifying process. It is carefully and brilliantly written, but even so the writer questions the value of the written word. Language is denounced as being approximate, a clumsy instrument able just to cut off a flat slice from the multi-dimensional item of reality which, if it is to be apprehended accurately and in all its fullness, requires non-linguistic modes of expression such as tone of voice, gesture, etc.[1]

La Rochefoucauld's scepticism about the reliability of words thus goes much deeper than his questioning of the labels currently affixed to human actions, registered in such maxims as (my italics):

Ce qu'on *nomme* libéralité n'est que... (263)

or

Si l'on avait ôté à ce qu'on *appelle* force... (M.P., 32)

It seems to extend to all the terms he has to use.

He was certainly taking risks in using blunt instruments for a delicate probing into man's innermost reactions, including the risk that his reader would not or could not follow him all the way. It is not surprising that we should hesitate now and then about the meaning of a term. What is much more extraordinary is that La Rochefoucauld manages to take us so far along with him and to communicate so forcibly the strange hidden idiosyncrasies of human nature.

Among the words which have attracted most attention are *intérêt* and *amour-propre*, the latter being defined by La Rochefoucauld at the beginning of a famous passage as 'L'amour-propre est l'amour de soi-même et de toutes choses pour soi.' (M.S., 1. The whole passage is given on pp. 86–7.)

The words have appeared to provide the key to the central

---

[1] This idea that tone of voice, facial expressions, gesture are best able to individualize the various facets of our psychological life is found also in maxim 255: Tous les sentiments ont chacun un ton de voix, des gestes et des mines qui leur sont propres. Et ce rapport, bon ou mauvais, agréable ou désagréable, est ce qui fait que les personnes plaisent ou déplaisent.

preoccupation of the author and for many readers La Roche-foucauld is essentially the writer who stated over and over again that everything in man springs from self-interest. This, they think, is a hypothetical theory, so we are free to agree or disagree with it, to accept it entirely or, for preference, partially. Excuses and explanations for such a 'one-sided' opinion on human nature are usually found in the writer's pessimistic temperament or in the accidental circumstances of his life.

To suggest that the whole edifice of the *Maximes* rests on a doubtful hypothesis or personal theory of the author is, I think, a serious misconception, and one so tenacious that it is necessary to say again what has been said more cautiously by other commentators. La Rochefoucauld is not propounding a theory; he is starting from a fact, a biological fact;[1] though one which, admittedly, our mental habits, our social condi-tioning (by which I mean the idealistic outlook society imposes on us for very good reasons) lead us to disregard or to distort.

Self-centredness is the basic and necessary condition of our existence. As far as our body is concerned it is obvious. If you are thirsty my drinking a glass of water will not quench your thirst; if I hurt myself you will not feel the pain. It is not difficult, either, to see that the reactions of the young child or of the completely uncivilised man (when we imagine such a being) are entirely conditioned by the need to gratify his self.

The picture becomes hazier when we consider man as a social being. Society is impossible if each man is allowed to indulge to the full all the impulses of his self-interest. As far back as we can go, society, in one form or another, has established a series of moral values destined to counteract the instinctive reactions of the self. Whatever they are (constancy, chastity, abnegation, and so on) their salient characteristic is that they are the exact opposite to what man naturally is. These artificially created values have been enforced by society by

---

[1] W. G. Moore has used a similar expression, giving it a slightly different slant and without personal commitment: 'For La Rochefoucauld *amour-propre* is not a vice so much as a biological factor in the human make-up' (in *French Classical Literature*, O.U.P., 1961, p. 128). See also the pages devoted to self-interest in his book on La Rochefoucauld (op. cit., particularly pp. 78–9).

different means, the crudest being of course fear of punishment. But in the civilised man these moral values work in a more subtle manner; they are presented to him as good things, and it is therefore in his interest to acquire them or at least to pretend that he owns them. Self-interest is here working at another level; accordingly men at times act in ways which are diametrically opposed to the way in which they would act if prompted by their instinctive impulses. Enlightened self-interest can depart very far from its primary biological reactions. It can extend in a very broad way; whereas for instance self-interest at some primitive stage would not go beyond the family, the civilised man may reach the point where his self-interest is closely bound up with that of humanity. But it is, I think, impossible to deny that whatever the degree of extension our self can achieve it is always there as the prime and central motivation of all our actions.[1]

This basic characteristic of self-centredness in man was no discovery of La Rochefoucauld. It had been acknowledged by many previous thinkers and theologians. For the latter it raised important questions. Was *amour-propre* a fundamental quality of human nature of such value that self-hatred was man's most wretched state? To what extent could it be compatible with love of God? Was it the source of all evil, the ineradicable mark of original sin, the consequence of the Fall? These problems were much debated in the seventeenth century, and A. Levi proves conclusively that La Rochefoucauld could not have been unaware of the theological overtones attached to the word *amour-propre* or of the pejorative sense it had acquired in Port-Royal circles and elsewhere.[2]

In fact, the Christian connotation of the word is visible in one of the posthumous maxims:

Dieu a permis, pour punir l'homme du péché originel, qu'il se fît un dieu de son amour-propre pour en être tourmenté dans toutes les actions de sa vie. (M.P., 22)

---

[1] Even the most self-denying charity of the Christian will not permit him to endanger or give away his most precious possession, personal salvation.

[2] Op. cit., pp. 225–33.

However, the *Maximes* are not the work of a theologian nor of a Christian apologist. A parallel with Pascal would be irrelevant or would at most prove that the content of the *Pensées* and that of the *Maximes* move in two opposite directions.[1] The theological overtones of *amour-propre* may affect our interpretation of the *Maximes*; they did not necessarily impede La Rochefoucauld when he focussed his attention not so much on the existence of *amour-propre* as on the way it works. We shall never know at what point it occurred to him – if it did at all – that the limitations set to human mental processes could be perceived outside a religious context as well as inside. His removal of maxims which had a religious import may be significant or it may not. It may have been dictated by purely esthetic considerations, a matter of taste, and a wish to preserve a certain unity of tone in the work.

What is evident is that La Rochefoucauld was intellectually fascinated by the difficulty of analysing and clarifying the exact nature of this self-love as a basic constituent of our psychological life. The superb passage entirely devoted to describing the elusive characteristics of *amour-propre* (M.S., 1) is well known and I shall come back to it several times. It is also very apparent that for La Rochefoucauld the relations between *amour-propre* and human behaviour were infinitely more complicated and problematical than the schematic picture of the working of self-interest and enlightened self-interest I gave, for clarity's sake, a moment ago.

The first proof of this is the distinction he tried to make between *amour-propre* and *intérêt*. I am substantially in agreement with W. G. Moore as to the difference of meaning between the two words. Moore takes as the basis of his argument the very fine maxim in which La Rochefoucauld compares *amour-propre* to a body, deprived of vital spirit, blind and deaf to the world, and yet coming to life almost miraculously when touched by the right stimulus of its *intérêt* (M.P., 26).[2]

---

[1] One might say that Pascal moves from a non-theological study of man to a theological conclusion; the reverse would be true of La Rochefoucauld who may have started from a theological concept of *amour-propre* and moved towards a non-religious study of man.

[2] I refer the reader to W. G. Moore's comments which go beyond the problem of terminology and rightly stress the stylistic achievement of this maxim (op. cit., pp. 97–9).

But though I accept Dr Moore's conclusions I think that the distinction between the two terms emerges even more clearly if we consider other maxims as well. The word *intérêt* is used in several maxims to imply self-advantage, usefulness:

Il y a diverses sortes de curiosité: l'une d'intérêt, qui nous porte à désirer d'apprendre ce qui nous peut être utile, et l'autre d'orgueil, qui vient du désir de savoir ce que les autres ignorent. (173)

The kind of *intérêt* in question may be specified: in the negotiation of a piece of business the *intérêt* of finding a successful solution can transcend the personal *intérêt* of the friends involved in the matter (278). The word is sometimes used in the plural as the criterion of utility and can apply to several things, simultaneously or in succession (our *intérêts* are not stable: 'le temps qui change l'humeur et les intérêts' (*Réflexions Diverses*, XVI, p. 223). Certainly *intérêt*, with this meaning of positive advantages to be gained by the self, is a powerful incentive to rouse the latent vigour of our *amour-propre*, but it is far from being the only one. It is often coupled with other elements:

Quelque prétexte que nous donnions à nos afflictions, ce n'est souvent que l'intérêt et la vanité qui les causent. (232)

or even opposed to a stronger element of our make-up:

On renonce plus aisément à son intérêt qu'à son goût. (390)

Amour-propre is not always activated by what is advantageous; quite the opposite:

...on le voit quelquefois travailler avec le dernier empressement, et avec des travaux incroyables, à obtenir des choses qui ne lui sont point avantageuses, et qui même lui sont nuisibles... (M.S., 1)

One may perhaps conclude that, whereas the meaning of *amour-propre*, self-love, is stable throughout La Rochefoucauld's writings, the term *intérêt* appears to be more flexible, assumes different colourings and, as we shall see, a certain moral ambivalence. Let us simply say at this point that it is at times associated with virtues, and at times with vices:

Les vices sont de tous les temps, les hommes sont nés avec de l'intérêt, de la cruauté et de la débauche... (*Réflexions Diverses*, XIX, p. 239)

or in the following maxim which is particularly relevant here since, while we know that the existence of *amour-propre* in each of us is for La Rochefoucauld axiomatic, that of *intérêt*, it appears, is not:

Il y a encore plus de gens sans intérêt que sans envie. (486)

An important part of the *Maximes* is concerned with relating human behaviour to *amour-propre*, commenting therefore not on actions but on motives. But it is not just a question of wrenching the mask from the face of civilised man and finding the instinctive self-centredness underneath. The problems encountered when trying to elucidate the relations between *amour-propre* and *intérêt* give an inkling of the complexity of La Rochefoucauld's undertaking. This probing into the inner man is the more difficult in that it goes against the natural way in which our intellect works, prompted by self-love and bent upon explaining itself in gratifying terms.

Not only does *amour-propre* do its best to hide from us its own workings; it also tries to conceal from our knowledge many features of that mysterious machine which, for lack of a better term, we call human nature.

The superficial view that La Rochefoucauld's main concern is the repetitive denunciation of self-interest collapses when we realise the variety of his explorations.[1]

---

[1] The most brilliant attack on this superficial interpretation remains Jean Starobinski's article 'Complexité de La Rochefoucauld' in *Preuves*, mai, 1962, which is one of the most remarkable pieces of analysis devoted to the *Maximes*.

PSYCHOLOGICAL INVESTIGATIONS

When we consider the amount of theorising about psychology which took place in the seventeenth century we can appreciate better the unsystematic and fragmentary presentation of the *Maximes*. The relation between body and mind, the study of the passions, the analytical survey of man's feelings and emotions had ranged from the very serious and coherent *Traité des Passions* by Descartes to the equally coherent but more frivolous *Carte de Tendre*. The tentative nature of La Rochefoucauld's approach to psychology stands out as something altogether different. There is no question of mapping a 'pays de l'amour-propre' where the 'terres inconnues' (3) stretch to infinity. 'Mapping' anyhow is the wrong image, as it conveys the idea of stretching out the substance of the mind and pinning down its characteristics on a flat surface. It does not fit in with the verticality and casualness of La Rochefoucauld's method, which proceeds by random soundings, at various levels, in a form of exploration rather similar to that of Montaigne:

Car je ne voy le tout de rien. Ne font pas, ceux qui promettent de nous le faire veoir. De cent membres et visages qu'a chaque chose, j'en prends un tantost à lecher seulement, tantost à effleurer, et parfois à pincer justqu'à l'os. J'y donne une poincte, non pas le plus largement, mais le plus profondement que je sçay. (*Essais*, I, L)

In some other respects La Rochefoucauld's study of man may also remind us of Montaigne. I am thinking of its subjectivity. The anonymity of the epigrammatic form is deceptive. It is true that we do not find the 'je' in the *Maximes*, but instead 'les hommes', 'on', 'nous', or at times, but rarely, a human group from which the author is obviously excluded – 'les femmes', 'les méchants'. Yet the starting-point of the exploration is undoubtedly the observer's own experience, and the depth reached by each maxim depends very much on the greater or lesser immediacy of the experience and on the degree of introspection involved in the process. This is an important feature of the book and I shall come back to it.

This does not imply of course that biographical criticism would be the easiest approach to the *Maximes*. The 'je' of a writer, either explicitly revealed on paper or camouflaged, is not easily perceptible through the trappings of the external data we possess; even less so in the case of an author who, like La Rochefoucauld – and like Montaigne too – tried to achieve, through his own experience, a picture of the human condition.

THE MIND AS A COMPUTER?
Patterns

However fragmentary the picture is going to be, there is certainly in the book an attempt to look for some kinds of pattern.

The first, the most obvious, is the physical or rather physiological pattern which is closely related to our mental make-up and our behaviour. The power of our intellect is dependent on the state of our body:

La force et la faiblesse de l'esprit sont mal nommées; elles ne sont en effet que la bonne ou la mauvaise disposition des organes du corps. (44)

The same is true of the reactions of our sensibility:

Toutes les passions ne sont autre chose que les divers degrés de la chaleur, et de la froideur, du sang. (M.S., 2)

Such statements are in keeping with the scientifico-philosophical theories of the times just as La Rochefoucauld's references to *humeurs*[1] are in keeping with current classifications of temperaments according to the prevalence of a given 'humour'.

---

[1] At least when the word is used in the plural. It appears more often in the singular with variable connotations, including that of mood.

The interesting point is that the physiological pattern is at the same time firmly acknowledged and yet considered an unrewarding field for further investigation. The opacity of the body will keep its workings secret and there is an unmistakable note of ruefulness in the following maxim:

Les humeurs du corps ont un cours ordinaire et réglé, qui meut et tourne imperceptiblement notre volonté; elles roulent ensemble et exercent successivement un empire secret en nous: de sorte qu'elles ont une part considérable à toutes nos actions, sans que nous le puissions connaître. (297)

This is very different from boldly stating that a man has a melancholy temperament if bile is the prevalent humour in his body – a superficial explanation which misses the essential point. The maxim suggests complicated and coordinated movements inside our body, the more relevant to a satisfactory explanation of our actions in that they constitute an orderly pattern: 'un cours ordinaire et réglé'. The rhythm of the sentence, the slowing-up effect produced by the long adverbs qualifying the verbs of motion, give an impression of harmony and regal assurance. And the end of the maxim is almost self-contradictory in its expression of utter frustration.

All we can perceive is that there is a 'forme maîtresse', to use Montaigne's term, of the body and the mind which conditions our reactions and which reveals itself even in our youth:

Il n'y a guère de personnes qui dans le premier penchant de l'âge ne fassent connaître par où leur corps et leur esprit doivent défaillir. (222)

The 'défaillir' is significant. In Montaigne the 'forme maîtresse' was viewed with more optimism; it was our genuine self, the only safe guide for a well regulated life, something to be treated with respect by educationists, and even something to be enjoyed.

At first sight, there is little room left in the *Maximes* for manœuvring inside this pre-determined pattern, and the stress is on its ruthless sway over us.

Not only are our mental reactions determined at the start, but, once set going, they follow a certain course which cannot be altered or reversed by our own will. We like to think that we can keep in check the natural evolution of our passions, but they evolve according to a process of their own which we cannot change. We are never 'en liberté d'aimer, ou de cesser d'aimer' (M.S., 62). We cannot love a second time what we have ceased to love (286).

The pattern which conditions us is not just the static pattern we are born with but the dynamic pattern which carries us along, though we have the illusion that we move of our own motion: 'L'homme croit souvent se conduire lorsqu'il est conduit... (43)

We think, for instance, that at a certain time we chose such and such a vice when in reality it was choosing us, waiting for us at the time appointed by the laws which regulate our life:

On peut dire que les vices nous attendent dans le cours de la vie comme des hôtes chez qui il faut successivement loger; et je doute que l'expérience nous les fit éviter s'il nous était permis de faire deux fois le même chemin. (191)

We are the prisoners of time, isolated and tied down to what is at a given moment the present stage in our evolution. We cannot recapture the past, not even a most precious experience such as the first ecstasy of the beginning of love:

Il y a une première fleur d'agrément et de vivacité dans l'amour qui passe insensiblement, comme celle des fruits; ce n'est la faute de personne; c'est seulement la faute du temps. (*Réflexions Diverses*, XVII, p. 222)

Nor can we anticipate the future and be ready to face it. As the pattern is not of our own making, we are at every stage confronted by a situation which is new to us, and what we call our experience is of little use to us:

Nous arrivons tout nouveaux aux divers âges de la vie, et nous y manquons souvent d'expérience malgré le nombre des années. (405)

All this implies strict limitations to the human condition, but La Rochefoucauld is certainly not satisfied with a mere endorsement of determinism. Even if our psychological life is, so to speak, 'programmed', La Rochefoucauld is well aware that the hidden mechanism is not simple, and probably suspects that it does not always work very well.

It seems that some of his soundings have revealed the presence of conflicting under-currents, of antagonistic elements which compose rather unstable patterns.

I am strongly tempted to think that the couple *force–paresse* might constitute one of these patterns.

Part of the difficulty here is the problem of vocabulary I mentioned in the preceding chapter. The moral connotation of a word, more or less perceptible, but obvious in the case of *paresse*, confuses the issue, although one may suspect that in a great number of maxims a given word works at two levels at once, and is used at the same time to express a moral judgement and as a tool for objective investigation of the psyche.

As a rule *force* is supposed to stand in opposition to *faiblesse* and is often taken to be a distinct moral quality, as meaning 'force d'âme'. Paul Bénichou has no hesitation in opting for this interpretation in the following maxim:

Si on avait ôté à ce qu'on appelle force le désir de conserver, et la crainte de perdre, il ne lui resterait pas grand'chose. (M.P., 32)[1]

We may be influenced by the use of the word by writers such as Descartes or Nicole.[2] Not that the meaning of the word is absolutely constant in their works, but it seems to be related to *volonté* in Descartes, and may even suggest, in Nicole, the cardinal virtue of *Force*.

In the *Maximes*, however, the word appears on the whole to be morally ambivalent, with the unobtrusive and neutral colouring it has in everyday language. It represents some kind of energy which can be used for evil as well as for good:

[1] *Morales du Grand Siècle*, N.R.F., 1948, p. 101.
[2] I am indebted to Anthony Levi for exchanges of views as to the possible meanings the word could have for seventeenth-century thinkers. Lexicographical material such as dictionaries of the time have proved unhelpful.

Nul ne mérite d'être loué de bonté, s'il n'a pas la force d'être méchant... (237)

It can apply to the power of passion or be mentioned as the vigour of our intellect ('la force de l'esprit' – depending on physical determinants – in maxim 44).

We may also note that, according to the variants, La Rochefoucauld hesitated sometimes between *force* and *forces*. The plural of the word could not possibly suggest 'force d'âme' or a cardinal virtue.

The most interesting implication of the word comes in maxim 30:

Nous avons plus de force que de volonté; et c'est souvent pour nous excuser à nous-mêmes que nous nous imaginons que les choses sont impossibles.

This seems to imply the existence in us of some kind of life-force, of instinctive energy which is not to be confused with the conscious and deliberate decision to act. The possibilities offered by this dynamic power in us are not infinite. It would not be sufficient to enable us to follow all the dictates of reason:

Nous n'avons pas assez de force pour suivre toute notre raison. (42)[1]

But in several maxims La Rochefoucauld intimates that there are untapped sources of energy in us, that we have the means of achieving things which may well appear to be out of reach:

Il y a peu de choses impossibles d'elles-mêmes; et l'application pour les faire réussir nous manque plus que les moyens. (243)

They are out of reach because of an antagonistic element, which opposes this life-force: *paresse* (the lack of 'application' in the maxim I have just quoted is significant).

We think only of the passive characteristic of *paresse*. We imagine that it coincides with a peaceful mood. We make a virtue of it: moderation; whereas in reality it counteracts or

---

[1] J. Truchet in his footnote to this maxim remarks that Madame de Sévigné would have preferred it to be the other way round 'Nous n'avons pas assez de raison pour employer toute notre force.' This would suppose a different scale of values in our mental possibilities. For La Rochefoucauld it seems that man's strongest point is his intellect.

paralyses the energy which is our most precious asset. It affects our mind even more than our body, and our intelligence, activated by the power latent in itself, could stretch very far, if *paresse* were not there to stop it:

L'esprit s'attache par paresse et par constance à ce qui lui est facile ou agréable; cette habitude met toujours des bornes à nos connaissances, et jamais personne ne s'est donné la peine d'étendre et de conduire son esprit aussi loin qu'il pourrait aller. (482)

We think of *paresse* as something negative because we do not realise the part it plays within us: 'De toutes nos passions' it is 'celle qui est la plus inconnue à nous-mêmes.' No reader can fail to register the impact of this word 'passions' at the beginning of the long paragraph (M.S., 54) in which La Rochefoucauld describes *paresse* as a positive element in our make-up, and a most powerful one.

De toutes les passions celle qui est la plus inconnue à nous-mêmes, c'est la paresse; elle est la plus ardente et la plus maligne de toutes, quoique sa violence soit insensible, et que les dommages qu'elle cause soient très cachés; si nous considérons attentivement son pouvoir, nous verrons qu'elle se rend en toutes rencontres maîtresse de nos sentiments, de nos intérêts et de nos plaisirs; c'est la rémore qui a la force d'arrêter les plus grands vaisseaux, c'est une bonace plus dangereuse aux plus importantes affaires que les écueils, et que les plus grandes tempêtes; le repos de la paresse est un charme secret de l'âme qui suspend soudainement les plus ardentes poursuites et les plus opiniâtres résolutions; pour donner enfin la véritable idée de cette passion, il faut dire que la paresse est comme une béatitude de l'âme, qui la console de toutes ses pertes, et qui lui tient lieu de tous les biens.

Although there is always a pejorative moral connotation attached to the word whenever La Rochefoucauld comments on it, the moral colouring tends to fade at the deeper levels, where this strange passion is shown as opposing indifferently our vices or our virtues and interfering with our self-interest. There is in it an unaccountable quality which prompts La Rochefoucauld to a lyrical appraisal of the relaxation it brings to our mental faculties; it is like an irresistible spell, a 'charme secret de l'âme', and even a state of bliss: 'une béatitude de l'âme'.

These are strong words. With *paresse* as with *force* one has the impression that La Rochefoucauld's explorations reach the tantalising point where he can only surmise the immense resources of the mind, or question, with a feeling of wonder, the raison d'être of *paresse*.

He is certainly puzzled that states of violent activity and states of inertia alternate in us without apparent causes. The pattern remains mysterious. He did not go so far as to suggest that the two antagonistic elements may be necessary for the balance of self. We should not look for synthesis in the *Maximes*. Would a knowledge of the 'cours ordinaire et réglé' of 'les humeurs du corps' (297) have helped him? Some patterns of antagonistic systems discovered by modern science might have interested him, such as, for instance, the joint working in us of the sympathetic and the parasympathetic systems.

It is, however, clearly stated in the *Maximes* that, whatever the conditioning forces at work, they have a restraining effect on our reactions which might be a safety device.

Our sensibility can react only within a certain range:

Il y a un excès de biens et de maux qui passe notre sensibilité. (464)

The possibilities of virtuous or vicious behaviour are also strictly limited:

Il semble que la nature ait prescrit à chaque homme dès sa naissance des bornes pour les vertus et pour les vices. (189)

Very rarely, there are men who have what La Rochefoucauld calls 'une force extraordinaire de l'âme' (and I do not think this should be read as meaning 'une force d'âme extraordinaire') men in whom the life-force is more powerful. They are the heroes, and for once *force* is strong enough to follow reason:

L'intrépidité est une' force extraordinaire de l'âme...et c'est par cette force que les héros...conservent l'usage libre de leur raison... (217)

They can push further away than other men the boundaries which necessarily limit the field of our moral behaviour, at either end:

Il y a des héros en mal comme en bien. (185)

Chance and necessity

Will the unaccountable element of chance interfere with the 'programming' of man's responses to experience? Chance may assume several forms. The commentators on the *Maximes* usually relate it to the various external forces bearing on man and stress the importance of the theme of 'Fortune' in the book. It was a traditional topic, and some of the fatalistic flavour attached to it might have appealed to a writer who was so much concerned with measuring the limits ascribed to man's freedom of action. It is undeniable that references to 'fortune', 'occasion', 'accidents' (with the meaning of circumstances), 'hasard' recur throughout the *Maximes*. But we still have to assess in which way chance can alter the self and at which level.

The main role given to chance by La Rochefoucauld seems to bring to light some features of a man's personality so far not very visible, or hitherto hidden from others and perhaps from himself. It may be a sudden illumination:

La fortune fait paraître nos vertus et nos vices comme la lumière fait paraître les objets. (380)

or the discovery of unsuspected qualities:

La plupart des hommes ont comme les plantes des propriétés cachées, que le hasard fait découvrir. (344)

or an opportunity for self-knowledge:

Les occasions nous font connaître aux autres, et encore plus à nous-mêmes. (345)

This role is particularly striking in the 'making' of heroes. The maxim:

Quelques grands avantages que la nature donne, ce n'est pas elle seule, mais la fortune avec elle qui fait les héros. (53)

27

should be read together with the beginning of *Réflexion* XIV ('Des modèles de la nature et de la fortune') in which La Rochefoucauld comments at some length on the creative process which accounts for men such as Alexander, Caesar, Cato or Turenne. La Rochefoucauld does not here contradict his definition, mentioned above, of the hero as a man who has 'une force extraordinaire de l'âme'. Nature provides the necessary qualities. The task of fortune is 'de les [les qualités] mettre en œuvre, et de les faire voir dans le jour et avec les proportions qui conviennent à leur dessein'. Fortune is compared to a great painter who arranges all the details of the picture round the main subject in order to create a visual masterpiece. This is not really the remaking of the man, but the producing of the public figure of the hero.

It is often very much at the level of the external manifestations of the self that chance appears to play an important part, and it is not always clear whether circumstances can modify our mental makeup. Men will probably react to 'accidents' according to their own degree of worldly wisdom, the clever ones managing to benefit even from unfortunate events, and the unwary spoiling their luck (59). Or else, as stated in another maxim, which seems to express the opposite point of view and goes back to a well known commonplace, the lucky man will just be the passive darling of the goddess Fortune:

La fortune tourne tout à l'avantage de ceux qu'elle favorise. (60)

Can chance alter, if not our inner self, at least our behaviour?

Quoique les hommes se flattent de leurs grandes actions, elles ne sont pas souvent les effets d'un grand dessein, mais des effets du hasard. (57)

This is somewhat ambiguous. The greatness of those actions may refer much more to public assessment of their importance than to their intrinsic value.

One interesting point is the coupling of 'fortune' with

'humeur' as the two deities presiding over the destinies of man:

La fortune et l'humeur gouvernent le monde. (435)

external circumstances and the internal pattern of man's reactions thus having equal power.

The two forces seem to run parallel rather than to interact. There are curious similarities between them. Fortune has a pattern of its own, strangely reminiscent of the compensatory mechanism inside man which prevents extreme reactions:

Quelque différence qui paraisse entre les fortunes, il y a néanmoins une certaine compensation de biens et de maux qui les rend égales. (52)

The pattern of both appears equally baffling, and partakes as far as we are concerned of the same erratic characteristic, even more so in the case of 'humeur'.

Le caprice de notre humeur est encore plus bizarre que celui de la fortune. (45)

In some cases the two parallel patterns are so close as to suggest a perfect and improbable coincidence which verges on the humorous:

Il y a des gens destinés à être sots, qui ne font pas seulement des sottises par leur choix, mais que la fortune même contraint d'en faire. (309)

Fortune as another deterministic factor working independently of man's inner fatality is not, however, all the *Maximes* tell us about chance.

Fortune may influence us at a deeper level. It may improve our moral behaviour (perhaps our moral being?):

La fortune nous corrige de plusieurs défauts que la raison ne saurait corriger. (154)

There is even the suggestion that the good or bad tendencies which compose our self are so ambiguous and unstable that they may be strongly affected by circumstances:

Toutes nos qualités sont incertaines et douteuses en bien comme en mal, et elles sont presque toutes à la merci des occasions. (470)

But we may look for the chance element at an even deeper level in other parts of the book and, paradoxically perhaps, not in the maxims where it is specifically mentioned. I am thinking here of all the maxims which refer to the oddities of the self, to the unaccountable contradictions within us:

L'imagination ne saurait inventer tant de diverses contrariétés qu'il y en a *naturellement* dans le cœur de chaque personne. (478) (my italics)

Some reactions are unpredictable: weakness produces vigour, shyness intrepidity (11). The *forme maîtresse* is not altogether to be trusted:

On est quelquefois aussi différent de soi-même que des autres. (135)

The pre-determined pattern may go wrong, not because of external factors, but of its own doing. If the human mind appears in La Rochefoucauld to be a kind of computer, it is obviously not a very good one; it makes too many inexplicable errors and produces too many random patterns.

The respective parts played by chance and necessity in the most obscure regions of the human psyche, as perceived by La Rochefoucauld, remain impossible to assess and constitute one more element of mystery in man's make-up.

Intelligence and sensibility

For La Rochefoucauld the least mysterious part of the mind seems to be its intellectual capacity. He goes so far as to say that whereas it is difficult to know 'les qualités de l'âme' it is easy to know 'celles de l'esprit' (80). He even has a certain amount of faith in the possible achievements of the human intellect.

Undoubtedly the degree of intelligence we possess is, as we have seen, determined by 'la bonne ou la mauvaise disposition des organes du corps' (44) and some men are doomed to be fools and to act foolishly. But on the whole:

Il y a plus de défauts dans l'humeur que dans l'esprit. (290)

This may sound very relative praise. We find elsewhere more positive statements concerning the high qualities which can be detected in the superior mind.

The variants of maxim 97 ('On s'est trompé lorsqu'on a cru que l'esprit et le jugement étaient deux choses différentes. Le jugement n'est que la grandeur de la lumière de l'esprit...') show La Rochefoucauld trying to analyse what those qualities are: the scope of perceptiveness, the depth of insight, the faculty of comparison, the sense of relevance and finally the power of making a critical assessment of value:[1]

L'étendue de l'esprit est la mesure de sa lumière.
La profondeur est celle qui découvre le fond des choses.
Le discernement les compare et les distingue.
La justesse ne voit que ce qu'il faut voir.
La droiture prend toujours le bon biais des choses.
La délicatesse aperçoit les imperceptibles.
Et le jugement prononce ce qu'elles sont.

The same qualities are mentioned again, in a different way, at the beginning of *Réflexion* XVI ('De la différence des esprits') in the description of the 'grand esprit'.

This of course does not imply that the mind of the 'grand esprit' will always work according to this ideal pattern, as other things like 'humeurs' or passions will interfere, but nevertheless it underlines the potential assets of the intellect, as does also maxim 482[2] which states that, but for 'paresse', our mind could have a much wider scope.

Yet La Rochefoucauld's investigations into the workings of man's intellect are in some ways disappointing, but not principally, I think, because of the ambiguity of his terminology, although we may meet with some difficulties here. Words like *esprit, raison, jugement* had been used with variable connotations from Montaigne onwards. Books have been written and could still be written on the variations in the meaning of these terms, on their synonymity, divergence and the multiple connotations of each of them.

[1] See Truchet ed., pp. 407–8, Maxim 41 of the Liancourt MS.
[2] See above, p. 25.

31

In the *Maximes* one may say, roughly and with caution, that as a rule *jugement* refers to the critical faculty which assigns their true worth to things. *Raison* is the power of reasoning which seems to exist in all of us, even in women, whose innate 'coquetterie' can be checked by reason (241); and its scope stretches from basic common sense to a kind of wisdom capable of acknowledging the value of this rational faculty (105) (at which point it tends to overlap with *jugement*).

Esprit has been mentioned in this study as the word which proved particularly unsatisfactory both to the critics and to La Rochefoucauld himself.[1] I am not sure that the contradictions pointed out by J. Truchet – *esprit* and *jugement* being sometimes considered by La Rochefoucauld as identical and sometimes opposed to each other – are real contradictions. The apparent discrepancy is due, I think, to the fact that the word *esprit* is used with different meanings according to the context of the individual maxim. It stands either for the sum total of our intellectual make-up, or for the quality of being intelligent, or, in quite a number of maxims, for a particular gift of mental agility, wit. And in this last case it can be opposed to *jugement* or to *raison*.

L'esprit de la plupart des femmes sert plus à fortifier leur folie que leur raison. (340)

Il n'y a point de sots si incommodes que ceux qui ont de l'esprit. (451)

On est quelquefois un sot avec de l'esprit, mais on ne l'est jamais avec du jugement. (456)

Le bon goût vient plus du jugement que de l'esprit. (258)

The fact that *esprit* is used quite a number of times as referring to that superficial quickness and sharpness of mind we call wit, and that in the last maxim I quoted it appears in connexion with the concept of *goût*, is significant of the level at which La Rochefoucauld considers man's intellectual faculties. For the most part he seems more concerned with the outward manifestations of the intellect than with its inner workings.

---

[1] See above, pp. 11 and 12.

It is perhaps because the starting point of his investigations is the world outside him that he is attracted by the possibilities of defining and classifying different types of intellects, as in *Réflexion* XVI ('De la différence des esprits'). It is also what enables him to have tests for the various degrees of intelligence and to distinguish between 'grands esprits' and 'petits esprits' or 'esprits médiocres'.

Comme c'est le caractère des grands esprits de faire entendre en peu de paroles beaucoup de choses, les petits esprits au contraire ont le don de beaucoup parler, et de ne rien dire. (142)

The evidence is given in a social context, and a man's mental ability is perceived and assessed through conversation.

It is therefore not surprising that La Rochefoucauld should be interested in what he calls *habileté*, which is in fact the practical side of intelligence, intelligence applied to our dealings with other men. This form of cleverness, which achieves worldly wisdom by fair means, is not to be confused with a rather low form of cunning which goes under the name of *finesse*. It is not always easy, however, to distinguish between what constitutes *habileté* and the qualities of superior intelligence, and perhaps we are not meant to make a distinction.

La souveraine habileté consiste à bien connaître le prix des choses. (244)

This is also the most important quality of the 'grand esprit'. The good brain makes correct value-judgements. But this raises another question: what is the criterion of correctness? In human affairs the criterion is obviously worldly success and there is no great difficulty in the case of *habileté* which is concerned with practical matters. The difficulty begins when the judgement of value bears on other matters, for instance, when it concerns a matter of taste:

...cette sorte de bon goût qui sait donner le prix à chaque chose, qui en connaît toute la valeur, et qui se porte généralement sur tout: ...cette juste disposition des qualités qui font bien juger...(*Réflexion* X, 'Des goûts')

Here *goût* is identified with *jugement* (not surprisingly, if we remember the maxim quoted above: 'Le bon goût vient plus du jugement que de l'esprit'). Good taste consists in knowing the right value of each thing. But *goût*, so difficult to define, especially in the seventeenth century, is closely connected with the conventions of polite circles, with the standards of the civilised man of the times.[1] We are again back with criteria which lie very much on the superficial level of social life.

La Rochefoucauld, however, goes on insisting on rightness of judgement as the most solid quality of the intellect. It may well be that the ultimate criterion is not that of social values but that of truth, so that the 'esprit droit' is the mind which can see things as they are and the 'esprit de travers' or 'esprit faux' the mind which distorts reality. Truth may also be the ultimate criterion of taste ('La vérité est le fondement et la raison de la perfection, et de la beauté... (M.S., 49)) and of the superiorly intelligent individual ('sa pénétration...lui fait toujours découvrir la vérité au travers des obscurités qui la cachent aux autres.' (*Réflexion* XVI)).

So far, La Rochefoucauld's maxims or reflexions concerning *esprit* or *jugement* have appeared mostly concerned with classifying different species of minds and trying to establish for them a hierarchy of value. Occasionally he probes more deeply into the way our mind works and endeavours to find what generates in us the judgements we pass. In *Réflexion* X, 'Des goûts', he notes that whereas some people reach 'bon goût' by reasoning, others have good taste instinctively because their *amour-propre* and *humeur* do not affect the basic reactions of their intellect. This is an interesting distinction between rational and intuitive approaches, which of course presupposes faith in what La Rochefoucauld sometimes calls 'lumières naturelles' and in a kind of innate harmony between things and our instinctive reactions. Even more interesting from a purely psychological point of view is the suggestion that some

[1] See on this point J.-B. Barrère's study of this elusive concept with reference to Pascal, Méré and Saint-Évremond (*L'Idée de Goût*, Klincksieck, Paris, 1972, pp. 21–51).

of the creative power of our intellect works in a subterranean manner – in our subconscious mind we would say nowadays – and suddenly presents us with the finished product:

Il arrive souvent que des choses se présentent plus achevées à notre esprit qu'il ne les pourrait faire avec beaucoup d'art. (101)

Such a remark makes us regret that La Rochefoucauld did not explore further the rich field of man's intellectual faculties. It would undoubtedly be unfair to reproach him for not being Montaigne or even Pascal, but one cannot help noticing that he shows little curiosity about some important facets of the intellect: imagination and, apart from one remark on its subjectivity (313), memory.

In fact, whenever he is concerned with the inner man, what interests him most is the way in which our sensibility, our passions, affect our capacity for reasoning and for judging, usually for the worse, occasionally for the better.[1]

Sensibility is certainly the part of our hidden self which fascinates La Rochefoucauld; and of all the passions that the human heart fosters, one stands out in the *Maximes* as being the subject of the closest scrutiny: the passion of love.

Here it is evident that La Rochefoucauld is looking inwards. With sarcastic impatience he pushes aside all the loose connotations which society has gathered round the word 'amour':

L'amour prête son nom à un nombre infini de commerces qu'on lui attribue, et où il n'a non plus de part que le Doge à ce qui se fait à Venise. (77)

It is none the less evident that for him love cannot be over-simplified and assimilated to a mere sexual impulse or to the casual love afair:

Ce qui se trouve le moins dans la galanterie, c'est de l'amour. (402)

---

[1] This is the case with maxim 404, which seems a comment on maxim 101 mentioned above and suggests that passions can be a powerful stimulant to the intellect:

Il semble que la nature ait caché dans le fond de notre esprit des talents et une habileté que nous ne connaissons pas; les passions seules ont le droit de les mettre au jour, et de nous donner quelquefois des vues plus certaines et plus achevées que l'art ne saurait faire.

The definition of love he tries to formulate emphasises the puzzling side of that passion and the complex involvement of mind and body:

Il est difficile de définir l'amour. Ce qu'on en peut dire est que dans l'âme c'est une passion de régner, dans les esprits c'est une sympathie, et dans le corps ce n'est qu'une envie cachée et délicate de posséder ce que l'on aime après beaucoup de mystères. (68)

The tentative formulation is extremely *nuancée*, with an added touch of indulgent irony. It sets a careful balance between the brutal assertion of the self and the intimation of mutual understanding, between the intrinsic insignificance of the act of love and the sophisticated approach which gives it its value through delaying techniques and secrecy.

This indicates the kind of searching analyses we are going to find. We have always been told that love is a cruel passion; this is a commonplace of literature. But few writers have delineated with such acute precision the cruel laws which love by its very nature imposes on lovers.

The self-centredness which characterises all our psychological reactions is even more blatant in the passion of love than in any other:

Il n'y a point de passion où l'amour de soi-même règne si puissamment que dans l'amour... (262)

with the result that love will show itself hard and callous, and so prone to inflict pain that it might appear barely distinguishable from hatred.

It is also a self-torturing passion. La Rochefoucauld's superb passage on jealousy (*Réflexion* VIII 'De l'incertitude de la jalousie') would be enough in itself to prove that he did not consider love from a safe distance but wanted to communicate the actuality and the immediacy of experience. The analysis he gives of the state of mind caused by jealousy is a remarkable epitome of all the features of jealousy Proust was to develop in his novel (particularly in 'Un amour de Swann'): the complete distortion of the world around us where each slightest incident alters our outlook, the endless and carefully worked-out deductions constantly shattered, the moments of mental aberration, when our mind accepts two contradictory conclusions, the inextricable mixture of love and hate, of self-righteousness and shame, the painful impotence of will together with the indefatigable persistence in pursuing in vain a certainty which will remain for ever out of reach.

The frantic agitation of the jealous mind may correspond to a moment of crisis, but it is of the nature of love to be unceasingly restless: the oscillations of its constant movement are the very condition of its existence:

L'amour aussi bien que le feu ne peut subsister sans un mouvement continuel; et il cesse de vivre dès qu'il cesse d'espérer ou de craindre. (75)

It is also subjected to the general dynamic pattern which, as we have seen, determines the birth of our passions, their development and their death.

This is perhaps where the analysis is the most thorough. Not only does La Rochefoucauld comment on the short-lived quality of the first joys love gives us, but he also follows closely and, so to speak, in slow motion the last stages of the dying passion, the 'end of the affair'.

The lover whose passion dies first has the advantage over the other in whom love lingers dangerously on (417) and who does not realise when he is no longer loved:

C'est presque toujours la faute de celui qui aime de ne pas connaître quand on cesse de l'aimer. (371)

The wording is significant and gives a calculated shock: the weight of responsibility does not fall on the lover who has ceased to love but on the other, blinded by his feelings.

Right and wrong are measured by criteria which are in keeping with the inescapable pattern. Moreover the texture of the pattern tends to fray near the end. Jealousy can outlive love and the 'vieillesse de l'amour' experiences the cruel sides of love and none of its pleasure (430). Love has also a curiously sensitising effect on us, so that it is when our diminishing feelings for someone are still a half-living presence within us rather than when our heart is completely free that we are more likely to fall a prey to a new passion (484).

And finally, when passion is spent on both sides, what remains is the aftertaste of shame:

Il n'y a guère de gens qui ne soient honteux de s'être aimés quand ils ne s'aiment plus. (71)

The picture of love which emerges from the *Maximes* is not a comforting one. It never is in all the writers, poets or novelists who reject the idealistic or romantic conception of love, who see it as it is and who acknowledge that love is inevitably linked with suffering.

In the case of La Rochefoucauld the pitiless analysis of the experience of love may have contributed to the creation of the legendary figure of an author with a desiccated heart who was probably both fickle and unlucky in his own love affairs.[1]

This seems a very surprising assumption when we think of the importance La Rochefoucauld attaches to sensibility. He sees it as the most powerful part of our self. It constantly leads our intellect astray:

L'homme croit souvent se conduire lorsqu'il est conduit; et pendant que par son esprit il tend à un but, son cœur l'entraîne insensiblement à un autre. (43)

L'esprit est toujours la dupe du cœur. (102)

It is also the most mysterious side of our psyche:

Tous ceux qui connaissent leur esprit ne connaissent pas leur cœur. (103)

We can perceive in the *Maximes* a recurrent concern and longing for what La Rochefoucauld calls 'le véritable amour', 'la véritable amitié'. Whatever the strict boundaries of the deterministic pattern, even jealousy is not axiomatic and the intensity of passion can suppress it (336).

---

[1] See the editor's regrettable comment on Maxim 5 ('La durée de nos passions ne dépend pas plus de nous que la durée de notre vie') in the Pléiade edition: 'Apprécions cette maxime, d'ailleurs vraie, si elle n'est guère originale; les passions de La Rochefoucauld ont peu duré.' La Rochefoucauld, *Oeuvres Complètes*, N.R.F., 1950, p. 631.

In fact, La Rochefoucauld tries to go deeper and deeper into the human heart, looking for the most genuine feeling in us, for some kind of essence of love which would redeem a passion which appears to be nothing more than a depressing mixture of domineering instincts, cruelty, shifting values and hard self-centredness and whose ephemeral joys are doomed to fade according to a ruthless pattern. It is worth noting that once, in the *Maximes*, La Rochefoucauld yields to the temptation of going beyond the evidence, and it is in favour of man's sensibility:

S'il y a un amour pur et exempt du mélange de nos autres passions, c'est celui qui est caché au fond du cœur, et que nous ignorons nous-mêmes. (69)

La Rochefoucauld says 'if'; this 'amour pur' may not exist and, even if it does, we shall never perceive it. And yet the precision of the 'c'est celui qui' seems to assert the existence of such a love. The maxim is deliberately puzzling. It suggests, in self-contradictory terms, the desperate assertion that man can break through the pattern of his limitations and at the same time it ironically denies him the hope of deriving any satisfaction from it. Is it a protest against human bondage? A 'cri du cœur'? Perhaps, but, if so, ruthlessly stifled.

'TERRES INCONNUES'

The prison of subjectivity

The fact that the *Maximes* stress the importance of determinism in accounting for human reactions may give some readers the impression that La Rochefoucauld's analyses, by reducing the mind to a network of conditioning forces, inevitably oversimplify and debase man. The same reproach is sometimes directed against the modern scientist who studies the human brain. The truth is that all the discoveries concerning the mechanics of the brain fill the scientist with wonder and excitement at the incredible complexity of impulses, the innumerable varieties in the different mental organisations, for the possibilities of combinations in the patterns of reactions are almost infinite.[1]

We find something rather similar in the *Maximes*. When La Rochefoucauld considers man in general, it appears that all men are affected by certain basic elements which condition them: interaction of body and mind, interplay of *force* and *paresse*, 'forme maîtresse', part played by chance, working of self-interest within the framework of society, and so on. But, to begin with, the nature and character of these various forces which act upon us is difficult to assess or to survey exhaustively:

Quelque découverte que l'on ait faite dans le pays de l'amour-propre, il y reste encore bien des terres inconnues. (3)

The interlocking patterns of the conditioning elements offer an immense range of variations. Hence the paradox expressed in the following maxim:

Il est difficile de comprendre combien est grande la ressemblance et la différence qu'il y a entre tous les hommes. (M.P., 19)

General knowledge is not good enough. To have an exact picture of anything or anybody we ought to know all the details, which is impossible:

Pour bien savoir les choses, il en faut savoir le détail, et comme il est presque infini, nos connaissances sont toujours superficielles et imparfaites. (106)

The paradox mentioned in M.P. 19 is to be found every-where: unity and multiplicity co-exist in human nature. For instance, there is a passion, love, which in its fundamental character is the same in all men and yet different in each of them:

Il n'y a que d'une sorte d'amour, mais il y en a mille différentes copies. (74)

---

[1] '...the most exciting and satisfying discoveries are those that illustrate the real measurable difference between human beings. The more elaborate our experiments, the more clearly we appreciate the great range and beauty of human personality...'. W. Grey Walter, *The Living Brain*, Penguin Books, 1961, p. 20.

Pride is equally present in all men as far as their inner self is concerned, but its appearance varies, depending on what it brings to the surface, or the particular form it then assumes:

L'orgueil est égal dans tous les hommes, et il n'y a de différence qu'aux moyens et à la manière de le mettre au jour. (35)

It is more difficult to know 'un homme en particulier' than 'l'homme en général' (436).

The reactions of the individual man are essentially subjective. They are prompted by his moods and even more by the idiosyncrasies of his make-up, by what La Rochefoucauld calls 'les goûts'. Here the meaning of the word *goût* is different from the connotation we met elsewhere. It does not refer to the faculty of judging according to certain esthetic or intellectual criteria, and La Rochefoucauld himself has made the necessary distinction: (my italics)

Il y a différence entre *le goût qui nous porte vers les choses,* et le goût qui nous en fait connaître et discerner les qualités... (*Réflexion* X, 'Des goûts', pp. 201–2)

The *goûts* are the instinctive, unaccountable likes or preferences of our 'amour-propre'; the value we attribute to things is calculated by the latter according to its likes or dislikes (M.S., 1).

These preferences are so important for us that they can be a more powerful incentive than self-interest (390) and we are so attached to them as the most precious part of ourselves that, whereas we can bear being criticised for our opinions, we are violently irritated if our *goûts* are disparaged:

Notre amour-propre souffre plus impatiemment la condamnation de nos goûts que de nos opinions. (13)

Inevitably our happiness is 'dans le goût et non pas dans les choses' (48) and whatever joy love can give is entirely contained within the self:

Le plaisir de l'amour est d'aimer; et l'on est plus heureux par la passion que l'on a que par celle que l'on donne. (259)

41

Like Montaigne, like Proust, La Rochefoucauld emphasises the irretrievably subjective nature of our perception of the world around us. Other human beings are therefore impenetrable. There is no safe, logical means of accounting for their attitude to life. We may even suspect that what appears as a well-considered and objective choice was in fact dictated by irrational preferences:

L'attachement ou l'indifférence que les philosophes avaient pour la vie n'était qu'un goût de leur amour-propre, dont l'on ne doit non plus disputer que du goût de la langue ou du choix des couleurs. (46)

Moreover we cannot perceive in others qualities which are not part of our own inner pattern:

Il est de certaines bonnes qualités comme des sens; ceux qui en sont entièrement privés ne les peuvent apercevoir ni les comprendre. (337)

The inner man is a prisoner, isolated within his *amour-propre*, in a closed world which has its particular idiosyncratic requirements. What constitutes his personality is basically unknowable for other men and, conversely, he is at a loss to assess them.

La Rochefoucauld himself is a case in point, and I venture to say that the prison of subjectivity is more obvious in him than in any other writer. Although one may suppose that he would have subscribed to Montaigne's 'chaque homme porte la forme entière de l'humaine condition' as a necessary corrective to subjectivity, the solipsism of the *Maximes* seems to be carried very far.

This is very much linked with the feature of verticality which I have already mentioned. La Rochefoucauld's insight relies on introspection. The strength and also the limitations of the *Maximes* come from the fact that they are a study in depth and not in scope. Whenever the apparent reactions of his fellow human beings are different from his own, La Rochefoucauld can comment only at a rather shallow level. This, one might think, is unavoidable. Yet, in cases where introspection is impossible, imagination, stimulated by a certain amount of curiosity towards the secret mind of those unlike oneself, might hazard a few guesses. Not so with La Rochefoucauld. The analytical tool then loses its edge, skids and scratches the surface.

The most glaring proof of this lack of imagination and curiosity is to be found in the maxims on women. As far as women are concerned, there is no discovery, no probing beyond the traditional motivation given for their attitudes. They are implicitly considered as a group of beings belonging to another species, and I very much doubt whether they are included in the anonymous 'on', 'nous', 'les hommes' of the maxims which do not refer specifically to them. They stand apart, reduced to a few conventional traits: *coquetterie* (332, 334) and intellectual inferiority (340, 346). They are required to be young, beautiful and chaste. Love is however the only passion which can be tolerated in them (466) but even so, most of the time their love is not a genuine feeling but another form of *coquetterie*. This over-simplification of female psychology indicates that La Rochefoucauld remains on the level of social conventions. His clearsightedness prevents him from being blinded by an idealistic conception of woman, and we would not expect less from his intellectual integrity, but we might have expected more, at least some questioning of the doubtful role assigned to women. In the previous century Montaigne had done so with some perceptiveness and analytical subtlety in his essay 'Sur des vers de Virgile'.

In one maxim there is a note of patronising sympathy for the painfully inextricable confusion of values imposed on women:

Qu'une femme est à plaindre, quand elle a tout ensemble de l'amour et de la vertu! (M.P., 49)

This maxim is often quoted as providing the right epigraph for *La Princesse de Clèves*, and may indeed be apposite. But, however close the friendship between La Rochefoucauld and Madame de Lafayette, I do not think that her book owes much to the author of the *Maximes*. The art of the novelist which

43

in this instance presupposed an imaginative delineation of several characters was outside his province.

The reality he thought worth pursuing was to be found only in the lonely confrontation of self by self.

The elusive self

This is perhaps the most dramatic side of La Rochefoucauld's investigations, the deepest plunge through layer after layer of eddying negations to find a positive contact with the solid rock of our genuine self. However attractive, even in its very starkness, the traditional objurgation 'Know thyself', the *Maximes* seem to prove that the quest for self-knowledge is an almost impossible task.

The first element which constantly distorts the features of our personality is our passions. Their mysterious workings impose on the self violent shifts in attitudes and spurious colouring:

L'avarice produit quelquefois la prodigalité, et la prodigalité l'avarice; on est souvent ferme par faiblesse, et audacieux par timidité. (11)

Admittedly passions may at times bring to our notice some hidden reality in us:

Il semble que la nature ait caché dans le fond de notre esprit des talents et une habileté que nous ne connaissons pas: les passions seules ont le droit de les mettre au jour... (404)

But such moments of illumination are rare. Most of the time the effect of passions is to prevent us from seeing ourselves or even from suspecting the part they play in our reactions:

Il s'en faut bien que nous connaissions tout ce que nos passions nous font faire. (460)

If we stop to consider how far we have been carried away by the complicated and contradictory movements of our sensibility, we are appalled to realise how we have been led blindly from one opinion to its very opposite:

Rien ne doit tant diminuer la satisfaction que nous avons de nous-mêmes, que de voir que nous désapprouvons dans un temps ce que nous approuvions dans un autre. (51)

There is no coherence nor stability in our self and so at times it appears to us a complete stranger, as unknowable as other human beings:

On est quelquefois aussi différent de soi-même que des autres. (135)

What there is in us is perhaps not one self but a succession of imperfectly connected selves, born at every stage of our life, trying to mould their precarious shape on circumstances and as such pathetically vulnerable:

Nous arrivons tout nouveaux aux divers âges de la vie, et nous y manquons souvent d'expérience malgré le nombre des années. (405)

Looking for our self not only leads to unexpected encounters with a stranger, it also implies a constant struggle with a cunning antagonist who does his best to camouflage his true features. The climate of our inner life is that of self-deception: 'nous nous déguisons à nous-mêmes' (119).

The theme of self-deception is one of the major themes of the *Maximes*. It appears explicitly in all the maxims which state how easily we deceive ourselves (115), even at times with some pleasure (114), how careful we are to shut our eyes to truth (M.P., 11) and so on. It is implicit in the whole work which represents an unceasing effort to remove from the genuine self the innumerable disguises it unceasingly dons.

It is undoubtedly this relentless struggle which gives its particular dramatic character to the confrontation of self by self in the *Maximes*. And it is not conducive to happy relations between self and self. La Rochefoucauld could not be suspected of any form of narcissism. There is no suggestion, as is so often to be found in Montaigne, that introspection may be pleasurable[1] or that, whatever our shortcomings, we are, after all, our own best friend.

Here the self is more like an enemy. It is true that super-

---

[1] 'Moy, je regard dedans moy; je n'ay affaire qu'à moy, je me considère sans cesse, je me contrerolle, je me gouste...' (*Essais*, II, XVII)

ficially its talent for remaining invisible spares us some painful humiliation:

Il semble que la nature, qui a si sagement disposé les organes de notre corps pour nous rendre heureux, nous ait aussi donné l'orgueil pour nous épargner la douleur de connaître nos imperfections. (36)

But there is in us a basic uneasiness as we dimly realise that the relations we have with ourself are 'de mauvaise foi'; they are in fact based on suspicion and distrust, on the feeling that it would be dangerous to uncover what lies safely buried.

Ce qui nous empêche d'ordinaire de faire voir le fond de notre cœur à nos amis, n'est pas tant la défiance que nous avons d'eux, que celle que nous avons de nous-mêmes. (315)

Thus the self when we attempt to track it in the deep and dark recesses of our psyche reveals itself as treacherous and insubstantial, allowing no more than brief and futile, if tantalising, glimpses at what might be its true nature and then vanishing into unexpected metamorphoses and multiple disguises.

Where else to look for it? La Rochefoucauld pulls us back to the surface, there to consider another side of the problem: the effect of society on the self.

Dans toutes les professions chacun affecte une mine et un extérieur pour paraître ce qu'il veut qu'on le croie. Ainsi on peut dire que le monde n'est composé que de mines. (256)

At first reading this may not seem a particularly penetrating remark. We are quite familiar with the idea of people playing a part, and we may be tempted to concentrate only on the moral issue; have we, or not, the right to hide our true nature behind a mask? But before we come to ethical considerations there is a more immediate problem: this sharp distinction between the mask and the face will not do. It begs the question. We have to decide first what is the real man and what is not. It is not so easy.

There is a part of our self which exists only at the level of our relations with other people, whether we are conscious of it or not. Our courage may be entirely dependent on the presence of an audience (216). We are strongly influenced by examples of what other men do (230).

Some of our feelings, which we believe to be a basic ingredient of our individual sensibility, may be in fact, although very real, the product of a cultural background:

Il y a des gens qui n'auraient jamais été amoureux, s'ils n'avaient jamais entendu parler de l'amour. (136)

A society of men is a strange thing. On the one hand, as we have seen, men's perception of one another is drastically limited, subjective and fanciful:

Nos actions sont comme des bouts-rimés, que chacun fait rapporter à ce qu'il lui plaît. (382)

and we judge of others according to what is relevant to us or not:

L'amour-propre nous augmente ou nous diminue les bonnes qualités de nos amis à proportion de la satisfaction que nous avons d'eux... (88)

At the same time we are intensely aware of the presence of others. A great part of our life is in fact lived vicariously through the supposed reactions of others. We attach a considerable value to their opinion. And, whereas we would be very particular when choosing a judge on a trivial money matter, we erect our fellow human beings, whatever their jealousy, enmity or stupidity, into arbiters of our life and reputation. (268)

The 'être' and 'paraître' are hopelessly confused in us:

Nous nous tourmentons moins pour devenir heureux que pour faire croire que nous le sommes. (M.P. 40)

Self-deception becomes indistinguishable from the deception we practise on others:

Il y a de certaines larmes qui nous trompent souvent nous-mêmes après avoir trompé les autres. (373)

There are many occasions when our reactions are solely dictated by what is expected from us. In this respect it is worth

47

pondering on the end of the superb passage in which La Rochefoucauld enumerates all the hypocritical reasons which account for the tears we shed at the loss of someone dear to us:

...on pleure pour avoir la réputation d'être tendre, on pleure pour être plaint, on pleure pour être pleuré; enfin on pleure pour éviter la honte de ne pleurer pas. (233)

The last reason is the most interesting, and the most upsetting. We conform to the attitude set by social norms. The man who does not conform, who has not acquired those automatic responses is 'un étranger' among men, like the hero of Camus' novel.

One might go even further and wonder whether this vicarious self is not the most real part of us. Perhaps, as Kafka suggests in a gruesome story, we exist only as far as our existence is acknowledged by other people and our personality is nothing but the image they have of us.

I do not know how far La Rochefoucauld would go in that direction but what certainly emerges from the reading of the *Maximes* is the terrifying elusiveness of a genuine self which seems to dissolve into its own fictions or those of society.

3

ETHICS

The word cynical is often applied to the *Maximes*. It may be used as a synonym for disillusioned and imply no more than a certain lack of faith in human nature. It may also contain a harsher criticism of La Rochefoucauld, since the word carries with it, especially in French, a more disturbing suggestion: the cynic being a man who considers moral criteria totally irrelevant to his choice of actions.

Whether La Rochefoucauld's approach to the problem of ethics is negative or not has always been a much debated question. Opinions range from a suspicion of inner corruption in the writer himself,[1] or of at least a personal grudge against his fellow men, to an appraisal of the book as positively concerned with moral standards of one kind or another.[2]

There is no simple answer to the question. The complexity of La Rochefoucauld's views on the subject reflects the complexity of his psychological investigations. We shall find shifts in perspective, even contradictions. Here again value judgements depend very much on the level of experience chosen by La Rochefoucauld in a given maxim.

ORTHODOX MORALITY

La Rochefoucauld takes for granted the validity of the distinction between vice and virtue. There is no ambiguity in his repeated use of these two words. He abides by the categories

[1] Cf. Madame de Lafayette's spontaneous reaction on reading the *Maximes*: 'Ah, Madame! quelle corruption il faut avoir dans l'esprit et dans le cœur pour être capable d'imaginer tout cela.' (Lettre à Madame de Sablé, 1663, in J. Truchet's edition of the *Maximes*, p. 577.)

[2] On this question of La Rochefoucauld's moral scepticism one should read J. Starobinski's brilliant essay on 'La Rochefoucauld et les morales substitutives' (*Nouvelle Revue Française*, July and August, 1966) and the subtle refutation of some of his statements by E. D. James in 'Scepticism and positive values in La Rochefoucauld' (*French Studies*, October, 1969); also Louis Hippeau's *Essai sur la Morale de La Rochefoucauld*, Paris, Nizet, 1967, more particularly Chapter III 'La vertu épicurienne de La Rochefoucauld', pp. 75–97.

established by society: generosity is a virtue, i.e. a good thing, greed is a vice, i.e. a bad thing. Moreover he suggests that such a distinction is so basic in men living in society that no man is a complete cynic. Even those who are as far removed as possible from practising virtue never deny its value:

L'hypocrisie est un hommage que le vice rend à la vertu. (218)

Quelque méchants que soient les hommes, ils n'oseraient paraître ennemis de la vertu, et lorsqu'ils la veulent persécuter, ils feignent de croire qu'elle est fausse ou ils lui supposent des crimes. (489)

The existence of moral values is a fact in any society. But in the light of La Rochefoucauld's study of the inner man these values are submitted to a critical appreciation which makes them appear very different from our usual way of looking at them.

The first point which is stressed over and over again throughout the book is that they rightly apply to behaviour and not necessarily to motivation. We may behave in a generous manner; it does not follow that we are activated by a generous motive. Of course, as far as society is concerned, this does not matter; society considers practical results. That it needs specific moral values to deal with specific problems of order and harmony is underlined at various points in the work, and particularly clearly in the following maxim:

On a fait une vertu de la modération pour borner l'ambition des grands hommes, et pour consoler les gens médiocres de leur peu de fortune, et de leur peu de mérite. (308)

But obviously this difference between behaviour and motivation suggests that only a part of ourself deserves the praise of a good action, and a great many maxims reveal the kind of amoral, or immoral, feature in us which accounts for a praiseworthy deed or attitude.

Ce qu'on nomme libéralité n'est le plus souvent que la vanité de donner, que nous aimons mieux que ce que nous donnons. (263)

Notre repentir n'est pas tant un regret du mal que nous avons fait, qu'une crainte de celui qui nous en peut arriver. (180)

The intention which prompted good behaviour may have been thoroughly evil:

On fait souvent du bien pour pouvoir impunément faire du mal. (121)

What also characterises our moral values is that they represent ideal categories, and as such are either in flagrant contradiction with reality (for instance, the virtue of constancy: reality is change, unceasing modification of the self) or constitute a crude over-simplification of our actions and feelings which are in fact an intricate mixture of varied and often contradictory elements. This latter point is stressed immediately in the first maxim:

Ce que nous prenons pour des vertus n'est souvent qu'un assemblage de diverses actions et de divers intérêts...

There is probably no such thing as pure virtue or pure vice:

La parfaite valeur et la poltronnerie complète sont deux extrémités où l'on arrive rarement. L'espace qui est entre-deux est vaste et contient toutes les autres espèces de courage... (215)

The moral side of our being offers a composite picture in which vices and virtues are not only inextricably mixed but also interdependent:

Les vices entrent dans la composition des vertus comme les poisons entrent dans la composition des remèdes... (182)

One more criticism of those moral values invented by society according to an empirical outlook: although given as absolute, they are strangely relative. Society can turn a vice into a virtue when it serves its purpose:

Il y a des crimes qui deviennent innocents et même glorieux par leur éclat, leur nombre et leur excès. De là vient que les voleries publiques sont des habiletés, et que prendre des provinces injustement s'appelle faire des conquêtes. (M.S., 68)

This pitiless revaluation of human virtues has appeared to many people dangerously destructive, systematically unfair to makind and leading only to an attitude of moral nihilism. The negative side of La Rochefoucauld's pronouncements on

accepted values, underlined by the reductive 'ne...que' construction of the maxim is what strikes the reader first. It is
humiliating and painful to be told that you are not really brave
or generous, that what you considered to be a good action was
inspired by vanity. The mechanism of self-defence which La
Rochefoucauld knew so well comes into play to escape the
shame of having been found out and exposed:

Nous aurions souvent honte de nos plus belles actions si le monde
voyait tous les motifs qui les produisent. (409)

'Who calls me villain?'

It is perhaps even more disturbing to be made aware of the
deceptive nature of the good we admire and trust in other
men. Basically what the reader finds hard to accept is the
all-pervading presence of *amour-propre*, and for him the
picture of the human condition which emerges from the book
is no more than the multiple ugly manifestations of one
ineradicable vice, selfishness. From the seventeenth century
onwards such reactions, or similar ones, have tended to make
of the *Maximes* a dogmatic depreciation of mankind painted
evenly in the one colour, black. As a result the positive side
of La Rochefoucauld's views on ethics is often overlooked and
the shades of his judgements obliterated.

Is the picture so black? If behaviour is, up to a point, a
criterion of goodness, men do a great many good deeds. We
may even be filled with wonder when realising what self-love
can achieve. In this respect a number of the maxims can be
read in two different ways. For instance, take the following:

L'amour de la justice n'est en la plupart des hommes que la crainte
de souffrir l'injustice. (78)

The first reading is to see in this the denial of a genuine love
for justice, as we are told that such feeling springs only from
our self-centred desire to find some protection against
eventual injustice. But the maxim works the other way round
also if we start, not from the idealistic point of view, but from
the fact that self-interest is inevitably the basic motivation in

us. We then realise that what appears as an instinctive low form of self-protection may rise to a moral standard.

The maxim which often shocks most as seemingly pointing to an extreme perversity in human nature:

L'intérêt parle toutes sortes de langues, et joue toutes sortes de personnages, même celui de désintéressé. (39)

and which appears the most negative, is at the same time the most positive statement of the moral possibilities attached to self-interest.

The form assumed by many of the maxims, the symmetrical pattern which opposes and links behaviour and motivation, affords the possibilities of reading such maxims backwards as well as forwards; and this double reading is very much in keeping with the 'two-truth world' of human values revealed by La Rochefoucauld and with the precarious equilibrium of moral concepts in the *Maximes*.

A hasty judgement on the book may also disregard a most important aspect of the moralist's view of morality. The attentive reader notices that, although all our reactions are given as self-centred, they are not all morally equivalent. There is among them a hierarchy of values.

Bonté for instance may be of dubious worth when it is the result of 'paresse ou impuissance de la volonté' (237), of 'complaisance ou...faiblesse' (481). 'La véritable bonté', which is rare, is something else (481). La Rochefoucauld does not define it but gives us some inkling of what it implies: an innate strength ('...la nature nous donne la bonté et la valeur' (365)), which affords us the possibility of choosing to be kind when we could use the same strength to be cruel:

Nul ne mérite d'être loué de bonté, s'il n'a pas la force d'être méchant... (237)

We are not allowed, however, to forget that the superior *bonté* which actively works for the good of others springs from *amour-propre*:

Il semble que l'amour-propre soit la dupe de la bonté, et qu'il s'oublie lui-même lorsque nous travaillons pour l'avantage des autres.

Cependant c'est prendre le chemin le plus assuré pour arriver à ses fins; c'est prêter à usure sous prétexte de donner; c'est enfin s'acquérir tout le monde par un moyen subtil et délicat. (236)

Whatever the end in view, the means to achieve it deserves to be praised as denoting qualities of refinement in both intelligence and sensibility.

The comparison between two maxims on friendship illustrates also – in a clearer manner, if with fewer nuances – a difference of value between two possible aspects of the same concept:

Ce que les hommes ont nommé amitié n'est qu'une société, qu'un ménagement réciproque d'intérêts, et qu'un échange de bons offices; ce n'est enfin qu'un commerce où l'amour-propre se propose toujours quelque chose à gagner. (83)

The kind of friendship pitilessly described in this maxim (note the piling up of words forcing upon us the idea of trade, barter and trafficking) represents the crudest reaction of self-interest in human relations.

Nous ne pouvons rien aimer que par rapport à nous, et nous ne faisons que suivre notre goût et notre plaisir quand nous préférons nos amis à nous-mêmes; c'est néanmoins par cette préférence seule que l'amitié peut être vraie et parfaite. (81)

Here we have true friendship according to La Rochefoucauld. As was the case with *bonté* the genuine quality of this friendship is relative; it still springs from self-love but from a much more complex reaction and, through a sophisticated process of extension and transfer, achieves its distinctive value.

Whenever La Rochefoucauld speaks of 'véritable amitié', 'véritable amour' he does not deny the biological fact of self-centredness: he indicates the full extent of our possibilities within the inescapable limitations of *amour-propre*.

Some eighteenth-century thinkers, such as Vauvenargues or Rousseau, as we know, did not altogether accept these limitations. They preferred to assume that there were in man some natural tendencies to act or feel in a completely altruistic manner, without reference to self-interest. Instead of a scale of values which graded the reactions of *amour-propre*, they established a clear-cut division in man's make up, a co-existence of two kinds of impulses in the self: some selfish, the others altruistic.[1]

To a twentieth-century mind La Rochefoucauld's views appear, I think, more coherent and more flexible. If he denies the existence of pure goodness in the nature of man, he is far from underestimating the better achievements of self-interest[2] or even the aspiration towards the unattainable perfection of the ideal world, towards 'an amour pur' which is much beyond 'le véritable amour' and beyond our reach. One remembers maxim 69:

S'il y a un amour pur et exempt du mélange de nos autres passions, c'est celui qui est caché au fond du cœur, et que nous ignorons nous-mêmes.[3]

As we read the *Maximes*, La Rochefoucauld's survey of man's moral conduct reveals more interplay of light and shade. He notes that some men are born with a *forme maîtresse* which enables them to acquire moral standards in a more straight-forward way than others. For instance envy is both a vice and a cause of suffering for the envious man. Some individuals are born without any tendency towards this particular vice:

La plus véritable marque d'être né avec de grandes qualités, c'est d'être né sans envie. (433)

Some of the moral qualities which society requires seem to conform occasionally to an unusual pattern in a man's personality:

L'intrépidité est une force extraordinaire de l'âme...et c'est par cette force que les héros se maintiennent en un état paisible, et conservent l'usage libre de leur raison... (217)

---

[1] The terms used by the eighteenth-century writers to express man's innate tendency towards good vary, but one recalls here the well-known distinction made by Rousseau in his *Discours sur l'origine de l'inégalité parmi les hommes* between *amour de soi-même*, which includes an innate feeling of compassion for others, and *amour-propre*, a dangerous form of selfishness created by society and the cause of all evils.

[2] We may at this point recall the difference (mentioned in Chapter 1), which seems to exist between *amour-propre* and *intérêt*, the latter being associated at times with virtuous behaviour as well as with vicious actions.

[3] See Chapter 2, p. 39.

This is given as an exceptional phenomenon (*extraordinaire, héros*) but, although exceptional, this occurrence remains within the limitations of self-interest. There is no transcendental connotation attached to the word *âme. Force*, as analysed in the preceding chapter,[1] is not a virtue in itself. What is meant here is that in such men the self-centred life force is so powerful that it carries them forward, pushing aside other reactions of the self such as fear or similar emotions.

The moral ambivalence of the factors which determine man's conduct is also perceptible in the fluctuations of his moral sense when he is submitted to the direct pressure of society through education, example, etc. Upbringing may increase our basic self-centredness:

L'éducation que l'on donne d'ordinaire aux jeunes gens est un second amour-propre qu'on leur inspire. (261)

There is in us a strong tendency to imitation which may influence us for the better or for the worse:

Rien n'est si contagieux que l'exemple, et nous ne faisons jamais de grands biens ni de grands maux qui n'en produisent de semblables... (230)

As we saw before, so much of a man's personality is conditioned by the other men round him, by the impression he wants to create,[2] that approval or praise prompt him to act better:

'Le désir de mériter les louanges qu'on nous donne fortifie notre vertu... (150)

Self-interest can therefore be modified. But how far can the moral sense he acquires lead him?

Can we take into account La Rochefoucauld's suggestion in one of the posthumous maxims that man can realise the basically immoral features in his nature?

Une preuve convaincante que l'homme n'a pas été créé comme il est, c'est que plus il devient raisonnable et plus il rougit en soi-même de l'extravagance, de la bassesse et de la corruption de ses sentiments et de ses inclinations. (M.P., 10)

[1] See above, pp. 23–4.   [2] See above, p. 47.

This maxim was not published by the author and, as J. Truchet rightly points out, it has an unmistakeably religious ring in that it alludes to man's fall from grace. However, 'plus il devient raisonnable' seems to suggest at the same time that man's rational powers can enlighten his self-interest as to its moral shortcomings.

The *Maximes* are not the work of a Christian moralist. But when La Rochefoucauld considered the orthodox morality acknowledged by his age it was almost inevitable that he should remember the Christian teaching which had moulded it. As proved by the content of the work he published, it was possible to examine the human condition without religious or metaphysical reference. Self-love was a fact, an item of knowledge, not an article of faith. Yet, however cut off from its theological implications, one may wonder if it did not remain flanked by two invisible powerful shadows: original sin on the one side, regeneration on the other.

INNER VALUES

Examining the level at which hidden motivations meet the requirements of moral conduct obviously constitutes a most important part of the *Maximes*, but La Rochefoucauld's preoccupations with ethics go deeper still. Underneath conventional morality and even accepted religious beliefs, underneath what a man must do to participate in common welfare and also eventually to save his soul, stands the self-appointed tribunal pronouncing on the intrinsic value of moral concepts. The thinker examines their relevance not to society or faith but to himself. He chooses among them, discarding some, stressing others. The criterion here is no longer usefulness but truth.

I am not implying that La Rochefoucauld evolves a new code of ethics, nor that, to use Jean Starobinski's expression,[1] he substitutes other *morales* for orthodox morality. I only mean that, at that deeper level, we find interesting shifts of per-

[1] See footnote, p. 49.

spective, and also perhaps the centre of La Rochefoucauld's moral preoccupations.

A different way of looking at a praiseworthy attitude may reveal the inaccuracy of the conventional label. Faithfulness in love is certainly admirable but why call it constancy? In reality our feelings are never static and, as La Rochefoucauld noted in one maxim, love, like fire, 'ne peut subsister sans un mouvement continuel' (75). And what we love we can love only for a time. But it happens that we may fall in love over and over again with the same person, each time for a different reason. Hence the paradox at the start of maxim 175:

> La constance en amour est une inconstance perpétuelle, qui fait que notre cœur s'attache successivement à toutes les qualités de la personne que nous aimons, donnant tantôt la préférence à l'une, tantôt à l'autre...

This does not lower the value of false *constance*. Quite the opposite. Genuine feelings take the place of an unreal concept. The precious quality of this experience is the more striking as we realise the rare and subtle pattern of relations between two human beings which is required here.

If on the one hand an exacting concern for pinpointing the only authentic value may result in setting it off with unexpected paradoxical radiance, the same concern may reveal a vacuum underneath some values solidly enshrined in tradition.

Courage (*valeur*) is a topic which keeps reappearing in the *Maximes*, often linked with *force* so that one might be tempted to find in La Rochefoucauld 'une éthique de la force',[1] *force* being opposed to *faiblesse*. True enough, *faiblesse* is denounced as being more contrary to virtue than vice itself (445), the more deplorable element in a man's make-up in that it is the only shortcoming which cannot be altered in any way (130).

I would certainly agree with Jean Starobinski that La Rochefoucauld seems fascinated by *force*, by this potential energy in us which is the most positive asset of the self. It is perhaps

---

[1] See particularly Jean Starobinski's 'La Rochefoucauld et les morales substitutives' (op. cit.).

present even in those weak people who have not the willpower to use it ('nous avons plus de force que de volonté' (30)), and I see *faiblesse* more opposed to *volonté* perhaps than to *force*. Whatever its importance, I am not sure that *force* in the *Maximes* can be considered as a substitute for virtue. La Rochefoucauld's pronouncements on the possible superiority it confers on some men are often contradictory or ambiguous.

If, on the one hand, the hero's intrepidity is shown to be an admirable strength of character ('L'intrépidité est une force extraordinaire de l'âme...' (217)), this same quality is deemed to be an illusion in another maxim, as it does not stand up to protracted misfortunes:

Lorsque les grands hommes se laissent abattre par la longueur de leurs infortunes, ils font voir qu'ils ne les soutenaient que par la force de leur ambition, et non par celle de leur âme, et qu'à une grande vanité près les héros sont faits comme les autres hommes. (24)

These last words, which erase the distinctive mark of gran-deur, together with similar remarks to be found elsewhere in the work, constitute what Paul Bénichou calls 'la démolition du héros'[1] and for him this degrading of heroic virtues reflects the mood of the age. The wholehearted admiration for great deeds, the belief in self-mastery, have gone and are replaced by a sceptical attitude towards stoic models.

It has been suggested, however, that La Rochefoucauld retains from former times an aristocratic preference for some form of Cornelian greatness which belongs only to an élite.[2] It is indeed possible when reading the famous maxim 'il y a des héros en mal comme en bien...' (185) to think of Cor-neille's remark on the 'grandeur d'âme' of his criminal Cléo-patre. But to what extent does La Rochefoucauld consider that such greatness can compensate for moral shortcomings, or even justify them?

'Il n'appartient qu'aux grands hommes d'avoir de grands

---

[1] The chapter Paul Bénichou devotes to La Rochefoucauld in his *Morales du Grand Siècle* (op. cit.) is centred on this view and powerfully argued.

[2] This is the opinion of Jean Truchet in his preface to his edition of the *Maximes* (pp. lxiv and lxv) and he mentions as an argument Corneille's comment on the heroine of his *Rodogune* in his *Discours du Poème dramatique*.

défauts' (190). The maxim is ambiguous. The double use of the word 'grand', the striking beginning 'Il n'appartient que...' seem to suggest that the shortcomings bear, like the man himself, the stamp of greatness and acquire the positive value of a rare and special privilege. But the maxim could also be one more attack against the kind of superiority the world admires, showing, ironically, how this superiority goes with a moral inferiority of equal magnitude.

It seems to me that the only clear assessment of what real greatness, genuine courage, might be comes in maxim 216:

La parfaite valeur est de faire sans témoins ce qu'on serait capable de faire devant tout le monde.

This is the test at the deeper level where self judges self and where all the orthodox attitudes, stoic or otherwise, are not to be accepted at their face value.

Stoic attitudes are often tantamount to attitudinising and call for witnesses, as was the case for many illustrious examples handed down to us by the tradition of ancient philosophers. Although La Rochefoucauld's rejection of stoicism is in keeping with the temper of his age, I do not think it is necessarily conditioned by contemporary trends. Montaigne also had finally rejected stoicism in another century for reasons similar to those of La Rochefoucauld and, more particularly, out of the same concern for truth.

Both of them set the same limitations to what human courage can do. The greatest achievement of the stoics was to face death with complete serenity, and therefore it was of the utmost importance to prepare oneself for it. Neither Montaigne in his last essays nor La Rochefoucauld will accept this point of view. We all fear death[1] and can do little to prepare for it. La Rochefoucauld devotes a long maxim to the subject (504). Death for any man who clearsightedly takes in its implacable reality is 'une chose épouvantable'. How can one

---

[1] La Rochefoucauld's proud statement in his self-portrait 'Je ne crains guère de choses, et ne crains aucunement la mort' (Truchet, p. 256) seems in contradiction with the views expressed in the *Maximes*. I shall come back to this portrait, which belongs to another level of experience.

expect self-love to accept what must necessarily bring its own destruction? Men may appear to die bravely because at the last moment they try to divert their thoughts from the horror of dying. The example given by La Rochefoucauld is that of a lackey who danced on the scaffold before his execution. Montaigne takes as an illustration those one can see 'sur un eschafaut' praying desperately 'y occupant tous leurs sens autant qu'ils peuvent' and concludes 'On les doibt louer de religion mais non proprement de constance. Ils fuyent la luicte; ils destournent de la mort leur considération' (III, IV). We need a screen between the naked face of death and ourselves. Some, says La Rochefoucauld, interpose the shadow of glory, the hope of being missed and other fragile but helpful covers. Others are partly protected by their dimness of vision. Reason cannot help us when death is near[1] and we turn away our eyes.

Le soleil ni la mort ne se peuvent regarder fixement. (26)

Our attitude to death when the moment comes means very little. Montaigne's final assessment is that death is not an important issue. Let us leave it to Nature who knows better and concentrate not on how to die but on how to live. La Rochefoucauld banishes as useless any speculations on death:

Peu de gens connaissent la mort. On ne la souffre pas ordinairement par résolution, mais par stupidité et par coutume; et la plupart des hommes meurent parce qu'on ne peut s'empêcher de mourir. (23)

No more value is to be found in relation to death. However much human societies and their philosophers have made of it, it is a false problem, an irrelevance at the level of inner values.

On the other hand what is supremely relevant at this level is the value of the criterion which tests all moral imperatives: truth itself.

La Rochefoucauld's pronouncements on truth are strongly

[1] Montaigne noted the difference between an abstract and distant way of looking at death and the immediacy and the concrete proofs of its nearness: 'Je voyais nonchalament la mort, quand je la voyais universellement, comme fin de la vie; je la gourmande en bloc; par le menu, elle me pille' (III, IV).

worded although not always very clear. In the following maxim his praise is unqualified in more senses than one:

La vérité est le fondement et la raison de la perfection, et de la beauté; une chose, de quelque nature qu'elle soit, ne saurait être belle, et parfaite, si elle n'est véritablement tout ce qu'elle doit être, et si elle n'a tout ce qu'elle doit avoir. (M.S., 49)

From the evidence of La Rochefoucauld's correspondence it seems that the beginning of the maxim was given to him by Jacques Esprit, that he was first puzzled and then found it so admirable that he adopted it in an enlarged form.[1]

We may be puzzled too. The maxim has an essentialist ring and suggests a pre-existing pattern to which a thing must conform to achieve perfection. Primarily concerned with esthetics, it might lead to a discussion on *vérité* and *vraisemblance* in literature. It might equally have a wider connotation. The first of the *Réflexions Diverses*, 'Du vrai', endeavours to give more precision to this particular quality. The last part of the *Réflexion* again relates truth to a question of esthetics but the first three paragraphs of this short essay bear on *le vrai* in general, the hallmark of it being its stability and completeness. La Rochefoucauld compares the generosity of Alexander and Caesar who gave kingdoms to that of the poor widow in the Bible who gave her mite. He stresses the fact that the difference was quantitative and not qualitative: in both cases we have true liberal behaviour in keeping with the personality of the donor. As another example, the same quality of cruelty is to be found in the child gouging out the eyes of a bird and that of the Spanish king putting his son to death. What seems to interest La Rochefoucauld is the authenticity of an attitude, an absolute characteristic, which is neither lessened nor increased by the variety of outward forms it takes.

This is not altogether playing with abstract concepts and dabbling in the world of essences. This concern for authenticity reflects, I think, a deep-seated preoccupation with sincerity which is constantly present in the *Maximes* and might

---

[1] See the letter of Jacques Esprit, Truchet, pp. 542–3.

very well be considered as the centre of La Rochefoucauld's moral conscience.

I am tempted to mention Montaigne again, not only because for him sincerity was also a quality of paramount importance in his whole outlook on life and on himself, but mainly because both Montaigne and La Rochefoucauld found in different ways that the pursuit of this quality ran into almost inextricable difficulties.

The problem of sincerity has two faces: sincerity towards others, sincerity towards oneself.

Sincerity towards others belongs to the level of social relations. Presented as attractive by orthodox morality, it is not easy to practise and can have disastrous results.[1] It supposes, to be acceptable, other qualities of a different order, such as intelligence,[2] tact or taste.[3] La Rochefoucauld, as may be expected, underlines the self-centred motivation which prompts us to speak the truth – or at least half the truth:

L'envie de parler de nous, et de faire voir nos défauts du côté que nous voulons bien les montrer, fait une grande partie de notre sincérité. (383)

La sincérité est une ouverture de cœur. On la trouve en fort peu de gens; et celle que l'on voit d'ordinaire n'est qu'une fine dissimulation pour attirer la confiance des autres. (62)

He admits, however, that among the various reasons which might lead us to show ourselves as we truly are, there may be found some attachment to truth, some dislike of dissimulation. In this respect some lines from *Réflexion* V, starting with the same definition of sincerity, are interesting:

...la sincérité est une ouverture de cœur, qui nous montre tels que nous sommes; c'est un amour de la vérité, une répugnance à se déguiser, un désir de se dédommager de ses défauts, et de les diminuer même par le mérite de les avouer. (194)

[1] This side of the problem of sincerity was magnificently treated in Molière's *La Misanthrope* and perhaps with even more finesse in Marivaux's *Les Sincères*.

[2] 'Tout homme peut dire véritablement; mais dire ordonnément, prudemment et suffisamment, peu d'hommes le peuvent. Par ainsi la fauceté qui vient de l'ignorance ne m'offence point, c'est l'ineptie.' (Montaigne, III, VIII.)

[3] 'Mais quand on a le goût faux, c'est une triste qualité que d'être sincère.' (*Les Sincères*, Sc. XII.)

It is not absolutely clear whether this analytical description presents us with different possibilities, mutually exclusive, or mixed motivation; whether it reveals a fact or partly suggests an ideal of what sincerity should be. The moral ambiguity which thus lingers over our best intentions is not the only trouble. Good will is not enough. Sincerity implies self-knowledge:

Les faux honnêtes gens sont ceux qui déguisent leurs défauts aux autres et à eux-mêmes. Les vrais honnêtes gens sont ceux qui les connaissent parfaitement et les confessent. (202)

Here again we suspect that these 'vrais honnêtes gens' belong to an ideal which is out of reach. We remember only too well all the maxims which reveal the reciprocal effect self-deception and deception of others have on each other. Either:

Nous sommes si accoutumés à nous déguiser aux autres qu'enfin nous nous déguisons à nous-mêmes. (119)

Or, vice versa, we cannot show our true self to others because we dare not look at it ourselves (315).

In fact the real problem of sincerity is that of sincerity towards oneself. It is only in the solitary confrontation of self by self that the absolute value of truth can be treasured or ignored or rejected. If accepted, it becomes at that level a very large issue and may even shake the very foundations of ortho-dox morality. For this is the depth at which moral conven-tions lay bare the appalling contradiction on which they rest. On the one hand they include sincerity as one of the virtues; on the other their very existence is based on deception. They deceive us as to the reality of the virtues they uphold, they compel us to deceive each other in conforming to moral behaviour, they train us in constant self-deception. What is called sincerity is a parody of what the word means.

Sincerity is something altogether different for someone who has reached this degree of critical knowledge. It implies facing the truth, acknowledging the fact of self-love, and all the limitations of our human condition. It is the virtue of lucidity, a gratuitous virtue, with little or no practical value as far as behaviour is concerned. Self-centred of course, as it represents the ultimate intellectual satisfaction of our ego, it has a priceless value for it suggests the distance which separates man acting blindly through the impulses of self-love and man clearsightedly taking stock of his situation against the greatest difficulties.

It is not an easy virtue. It requires intelligence. The test of a powerful intellect is for La Rochefoucauld the capacity to perceive hidden truth:

...sa pénétration...lui fait toujours découvrir la vérité au travers des obscurités qui la cachent aux autres. (*Réflexion* XVI)

Given La Rochefoucauld's confidence in the human mind if only man would stretch his intellectual possibilities, this is perhaps not the most difficult requirement.

The main obstacle is that truth is essentially painful, and sincerity asks for strength. The maxim which states that:

Les personnes faibles ne peuvent être sincères. (316)

is particularly relevant when it comes to sincerity towards oneself. It takes a great deal of courage to face unadorned truth, to look for all the real features of our successive avatars and to acknowledge them. How many of us will be strong enough after the age of seventy to recognise ourselves in the picture of old age given in the long depressing passage 'De la retraite' (*Réflexion* XVIII)?[1]

This is what makes the reading of the work so often painful. So much so that some readers, even some critics, have seen in La Rochefoucauld a kind of wilful cruelty born of a bitter grudge against society and directed against it, while he himself stood immune, protected by the conceited assurance of belonging to a moral élite.[2] This assessment, it seems to me, can

---

[1] We find in Montaigne also a cruel picture of old age, faced lucidly and with remarkable courage: '...et ne se void point d'âmes, ou fort rares, qui en vieillissant ne sentent à l'aigre et au moisi' (see the last pages of the chapter 'Du Repentir', III, II).

[2] This is, in particular, the opinion of A. J. Krailsheimer: 'He [La Rochefoucauld] stands aloof and disgusted outside the society he condemns, and his own assumption of superiority is no less marked for being tacit' (*Studies in Self-Interest*, Clarendon Press, 1962, p. 96).

be supported only by the most superficial side of the *Maximes*, and is disproved by the penetrating force of the author's psychological investigations. The more piercing thrusts of the scalpel, the most hurtful, were necessarily self-inflicted in order to reach those inner depths that the mere observation of men and society round him could not discover.

If La Rochefoucauld in a way belongs to a moral élite, it is because of this kind of intellectual stoicism, somewhat similar to Montaigne's final position, which is implied by his acceptance of the humiliating reality to be found in the make-up of any man, and first and foremost in himself.

Not that he comes to terms with that reality with the spirit of tolerance and patience which is typical of Montaigne. We must remember at this point the struggle with the elusive protean reality of the self as with an enemy who knows all the most subtle tricks of camouflage. Thus the greater the humiliation, the more exquisite the pain. La Rochefoucauld's analysis of self-love may even lead us to suspect that this ultimate value, sincerity towards oneself, this pursuit of an ever-elusive truth was born of despair and built on impossibility. It is difficult to breathe for long in this underworld where lucidity tries to grasp the reluctant ego. The temptation is to hope against hope:

L'espérance, toute trompeuse qu'elle est, sert au moins à nous mener à la fin de la vie par un chemin agréable. (168)

and, leaving the awesome truth darkly reflected in the inward mirror, emerge into another world.

THROUGH THE LOOKING-GLASS

This is the world of a civilised seventeenth-century man for whom society and social life are inescapable facts. Every man – at least every man who counts – is involved in an elaborate game of human relations against the background of the drawing-room or the court. The more civilised the society, the more refinement is sought to make these relations as smooth and agreeable as possible. The part of each individual is to please, and to be pleased. The game has to be played in an atmosphere of civility, civility being a kind of social contract for the benefit of all parties, and it is both an obligation and a reward in itself:

La civilité est un désir d'en recevoir, et d'être estimé poli. (260)

La Rochefoucauld knows the rules of the game perfectly, appreciates the finer points; and a number of maxims as well as some of the *Réflexions* show his contribution towards delineating the ideal performer, *l'honnête homme*.

To surface into this world from the depths of moral concern is to come upon a world of inverted values:

Il y a des gens dégoûtants[1] avec du mérite, et d'autres qui plaisent avec des défauts. (155)

Vices can be an asset if they 'servent au commerce de la vie' (273), and moral shortcomings, well used, shine more than virtue:

Il y a de certains défauts qui, bien mis en œuvre, brillent plus que la vertu même. (354)

Truth becomes an irrelevant criterion:

Il y a des faussetés déguisées qui représentent si bien la vérité que ce serait mal juger que de ne pas s'y laisser tromper. (282)

the more so as the little good truth can do is more than cancelled by the evil caused by what merely seems to be true:

La vérité ne fait pas tant de bien dans le monde que ses apparences y font de mal. (64)

Intelligence is no longer at the service of truth. It takes the form of *habileté* which is primarily concerned with the furthering of worldly advantages. This implies the faculty of planning one's actions in a careful and orderly manner:

Un habile homme doit régler le rang de ses intérêts et les conduire chacun dans son ordre.... (66)

[1] Unlikeable.

It calls also for very subtle manœuvres, so that *habileté* easily becomes cunning *finesse* in a clever use of bluff and double bluff:

La plus subtile de toutes les finesses est de savoir bien feindre de tomber dans les pièges que l'on nous tend, et on n'est jamais si aisément trompé que quand on songe à tromper les autres. (117)

However, such a form of intelligence is not always an advantage. Its tactics place the *habile* in a vulnerable position towards an opponent who through stupidity or uncouthness does not follow the rules of the game:

Il suffit quelquefois d'être grossier pour n'être pas trompé par un habile homme. (129)

If therefore the outcome of sober *habileté* and calculated moves is precarious, why not at times throw all caution to the winds? A new value appears which is antithetical to rational judgement: folly:[1]

Qui vit sans folie n'est pas si sage qu'il croit. (209)

Il arrive quelquefois des accidents dans la vie, d'où il faut être un peu fou pour se bien tirer. (310)

The most important feature of this inverted universe is that the words and gestures of the performers should be direected towards the satisfaction of others, and not of one's self. The best example is given in *Réflexion* IV where La Rochefoucauld expounds at some length the art of conversation, showing how it rests for the most part on giving precedence to other people's opinions, feelings and personal idiosyncracies over one's own.

There is no doubt that this stress placed on the desire to please, and its corollary, reciprocal satisfaction, makes the picture most attractive. We might even include in it some agreeable views on love which are the very reverse of the harsh and pessimistic analysis of this passion I mentioned previously.

[1] Peter Nurse suggests a very interesting link between Erasmus' *Praise of Folly* and the seventeenth-century concept of the *honnête homme*, and includes La Rochefoucauld among the writers who, following the Erasmian tradition, rejected the cold reason of philosophers and considered folly as part of human wisdom. ('Essai de définition du comique moliéresque' in *Revue des Sciences Humaines*, January–March, 1964, pp. 16–18.)

I am thinking here of the text published by J. D. Hubert which he suggests was probably written by La Rochefoucauld: *La Justification de l'Amour*.[1] Love is depicted in this little treatise as a beautiful, noble and reasonable passion; the attitude of the lover is respectful and considerate. The long platonic or neo-platonic tradition which has been the fictional cover of any civilised approach to love through the ages is evident in the text, set up by a refinement in tone – falsely naïve, complimentary and subtly caressing – which bears the stamp of seventeenth-century urbanity. The importance of the tone, together with the punctilious delicacy in the lover's courtship, lights up the superficial and charming aspect of love, something perhaps which La Rochefoucauld was praising in the following maxim:

L'amour, tout agréable qu'il est, plaît encore plus par les manières dont il se montre que par lui-même. (501)

In a world where the unpleasant aspects of self-centredness are so carefully checked, and where truth has so little relevance, it is more or less axiomatic that one should wear a mask. ('Les hommes ne vivraient pas longtemps en société s'ils n'étaient les dupes les uns des autres.' (87).) And yet the supreme refinement of all is paradoxically *le naturel*.

Affectation is strongly condemned as bringing upon itself the worst punishment social life can inflict – to be laughed at:

On n'est jamais si ridicule par les qualités que l'on a que par celles que l'on affecte d'avoir. (134)

La Rochefoucauld's praise of little children who are delightful because 'ils sont encore renfermés dans cet air et dans ces manières que la nature leur a donnés' (*Réflexion* IH, p. 189) should not lead us, however, to think that this quality of naturalness, which appealed so much to the age, rests simply on spontaneity. We know that in literature it does not; one inevitably thinks of La Fontaine. In social life also it is a carefully thought-out creation which requires some mature experience of life:

[1] Texte présenté par J. D. Hubert, Nizet, 1971.

La plupart des jeunes gens croient être naturels, lorsqu'ils ne sont que mal polis et grossiers. (372)

On the other hand, such is the paradoxical logic of the world through the looking-glass that the worst affectation is that of trying to have none:

Rien n'empêche tant d'être naturel que l'envie de le paraître. (431)

It seems that one cannot win.

Nevertheless *Réflexion* III ('De l'air et des manières') is a short essay on the art of being *naturel*. The key word is *convenir*. The criterion of naturalness is in fact the suitability of the mask. This must be in keeping with the idiosyncrasies of the self: 'un air qui convient à la figure et aux talents de chaque personne' (*Réflexion* III), with age ('savoir être vieux'), sex, condition and circumstances ('on ne marche pas à la tête d'un régiment comme on marche en se promenant' (*Réflexion* III)). Naturalness does not exclude improving suitable qualities nor enhancing them with added graces such as politeness – a universally suitable addition – nor even culture if compatible with our innate talents.

Thus each man should create his own personage acceptable to others and agreeable to himself. The difference between this semi-artificial modelling of oneself and the real man is rather similar to the distinction, so dear to the literary theorists of the time, between *le vraisemblable* and *le vrai*.

Perhaps one of the best illustrations of such a re-creation of one's individuality is the self-portrait La Rochefoucauld offers to society, for public consumption. This is not exactly the writer as he knows himself, but as he considers it right to be known. The confession of his shortcomings is restricted to what is tolerable in an *honnête homme* and a man of his rank. For instance, it would be intolerable and *invraisemblable* to run the risk of appearing a coward by giving a limit to genuine courage. Hence the overstatement: 'Je ne crains guère de choses, *et ne crains aucunement la mort*' (my italics) in contradiction with his statements in the *Maximes* on the universal fear of death. It is in many ways a flattering portrait, dignified and elegant, and La Rochefoucauld would be the first to comment on it sarcastically:

On n'aurait guère de plaisir si on ne se flattait jamais. (123)

Elegance is inseparable from the golden rule, *plaire*, which governs the social world, and critics have rightly noted the preoccupation with esthetics which permeates La Rochefoucauld's *art de vivre*.[1]

One might say that naturalness is a question of harmony. It is significant that La Rochefoucauld should resort to comparisons with music to express what our manners should be, deploring the fact that nobody really knows how to 'accorder son air et ses manières avec sa figure ni ses tons et ses paroles avec ses pensées et ses sentiments;...personne n'a l'oreille assez juste pour entendre parfaitement cette sorte de cadence' (*Réflexion* III).

There exists a general kind of harmony which should be respected: to each feeling correspond a certain tone of speech, particular gestures and facial expression. The wrong tone, the inappropriate gesture are enough to make a person unattractive:

Tous les sentiments ont chacun un ton de voix, des gestes et des mines qui leur sont propres. Et ce rapport bon ou mauvais, agréable ou désagréable, est ce qui fait que les personnes plaisent ou déplaisent. (255)

This is very much like the stylisation of gestures and attitudes expected from a good actor and it is interesting to note that La Rochefoucauld had first included in the maxim: 'c'est ce qui fait les bons et les mauvais acteurs'.

It may also happen that this pleasurable harmony does not seem to conform to an acknowledged form of stylisation. It still has a harmonious pattern, but a pattern all of its own, mysterious and tantalising:

On peut dire de l'agrément séparé de la beauté que c'est une symétrie dont on ne sait point les règles, et un rapport secret des traits

---

[1] See particularly Jean Starobinski in the article on 'morales substitutives' (op. cit.).

ensemble, et des traits avec les couleurs et avec l'air de la personne. (240)[1]

Keeping in mind this care for a harmonious pattern, one might be tempted to say that for La Rochefoucauld social life is, rather than a game, a ballet, although unfortunately too many dancers have chosen preposterous masks and also the orchestra is not very good.

'INTERFERENCES'

So far I have considered independently three different levels of experience which account for the different and even contradictory values to be found in La Rochefoucauld's writings. But if these present us with what Montaigne, speaking about himself, called 'une âme à divers étages', it does not follow that we are dealing with tightly partitioned strata.

For instance, even if La Rochefoucauld's picture of the 'commerce que les honnêtes gens ont ensemble' (*Réflexion* II) is concerned with the ideal of *plaire* in society, his deep-seated attachment to truth comes at times to the surface, requiring a modicum of sincerity. Conversely, when playing his part in the subtle artificial atmosphere of drawing-room pastimes, he never forgets the distance which should separate those superficial human relations from the vulnerable hidden self; so that not only must one not let one's real self become enslaved by society ('il faut que chacun conserve sa liberté' (*Réflexion* II)), but one must also be careful when talking to one's friends about what will interest them most themselves not to penetrate too deeply below the surface:

Il y a de la politesse, et quelquefois même de l'humanité, à ne pas entrer trop avant dans les replis de leur cœur;...(*Réflexion* II)

This is the type of remark which gives delicate nuances to what might appear simply a worldly code of behaviour. We suspect at times a marked hesitation between an impulse of sensibility

---

[1] I do not share the opinion of W. G. Moore who finds the first of these maxims unclear (op. cit. pp. 25–6) nor of J. Truchet who seems to consider the second as one more banal expression of the fashionable 'je ne sais quoi'.

and a precept of worldly wisdom, a confusion – deliberate or not – between a moral concern and the demands of elegance. It is difficult to decide whether the semantic instability of some of the words he uses serves him well in these almost imperceptible shifts from one level to another, or whether it is a disadvantage since it confuses the reader.

The multivalence of the word *honnête* is well known. The context may indicate that La Rochefoucauld is referring to a moral quality such as probity or integrity, or to good manners, or in the case of women to chastity.[1] In some cases we may hesitate:

C'est être véritablement honnête homme que de vouloir être toujours exposé à la vue des honnêtes gens. (206)

As J. Truchet remarks in a footnote, the maxim makes sense whether we take the *honnête* in its moral or in its social connotation. But do we have to choose between the two interpretations? Is this not a case where, consciously or unconsciously, the distinction between two different kinds of qualities has become blurred or, more exactly, where one is superimposed on the other, so that to be an *honnête homme* in the full meaning of the word ('véritablement honnête homme') implies a perfect blend of both qualities?

The very word which signifies value, the word *mérite*, is one of which the connotations are most elusive. It often seems to imply an inner value, a genuine quality, albeit not specified (virtue? intelligence? courage?):

Le monde récompense plus souvent les apparences du mérite que le mérite même. (166)

although another maxim states that the *mérite* does not lie in the qualities themselves but in the way they are used:

On ne doit pas juger du mérite d'un homme par ses grandes qualités, mais par l'usage qu'il en sait faire. (437)

This is getting near the surface, and in some other maxims one might suspect that *mérite* refers to the good opinion the world has of a man:

[1] See Chapter 1, p. 10.

Le mérite des hommes a sa saison aussi bien que les fruits. (291)

but this may also imply that our good qualities are no more static than the rest of our mental makeup and are subjected to the same deterministic pattern of growth and decline.

Is the same ambiguity also to be found in maxim 474?

Il y a peu de femmes dont le mérite dure plus que la beauté.

Does it mean: we find moral or intellectual qualities in women only as long as they are beautiful? or does it suggest that most women do not possess any other value than their beauty so that when their good looks vanish there is nothing left?

The words *habile, habileté* would seem first to refer to the social and practical side of life. Even there the value of this form of intelligence varies. It is sometimes opposed to *finesse*, which is an inferior and rather despicable kind of intellectual nimbleness:

Les finesses et les trahisons ne viennent que du manque d'habileté. (126)

but we are also told that 'les plus habiles' are those who keep the use of *finesse* for worthwhile affairs while affecting to despise cunning (124).

The machiavellian flavour of this last maxim leads us to suppose that *habileté* may not really have any moral superiority, which is confirmed by the following opposition between *habileté* and *probité*:

Il est difficile de juger si un procédé net, sincère et honnête est un effet de probité ou d'habileté. (170)

Is it even necessary to be intelligent to be *habile*?

Il y a des gens niais que se connaissent, et qui emploient habilement leur niaiserie. (208)

Yet at times *habileté* is certainly associated with the penetrating lucidity which is such a central value for La Rochefoucauld:

Il n'y a guère d'homme assez habile pour connaître tout le mal qu'il fait. (269)

Can we find praise of this keen perception of truth and excellent judgement in maxim 244?

La souveraine habileté consiste à bien connaître le prix des choses.

I am not sure whether 'le prix des choses' refers to the true value of things or whether La Rochefoucauld is thinking along the lines of practical advantages and of how much they are worth our trouble.

There are cases where the shift in meaning of these words *habileté, habile* is deliberately used by La Rochefoucauld, and he plays on it to produce a clever antithesis:

La plus grande habileté des moins habiles est de se savoir soumettre à la bonne conduite d'autrui. (M.S., 60)

This of course raises another question: was the content of a maxim at times dictated by the wish to produce an unexpected paradox, a striking epigram?

We shall soon come to the question of La Rochefoucauld's artistic achievement. Meanwhile we are left with what is in many ways an inconclusive survey of La Rochefoucauld's approach, or rather approaches to ethics. The different values, the interferences between various channels of experience are not to be attributed only to the unsystematic nature of the work. They suggest the incessant movements of a thought in a multidimensional world of its own where sentences can work backwards, pictures reverse, verticality may stop being a straight line and parallels may meet.[1]

---

[1] One would, I think, willingly agree with J. Truchet when he asks that La Rochefoucauld should be granted the right to be ambiguous, hesitant and self-contradictory. (Introduction, pp. lxxi and lxxii.)

4

ART

La Rochefoucauld's stylistic achievement in the *Maximes* has always been praised. W. G. Moore notes that even the 'accessory qualities of epigram – the pleasures of sound and rhythm' are to be found in the work and he illustrates the point very convincingly.[1] Choice of words, patterns such as antithesis or comparison, images, etc. have been commented upon, classified. Indeed the survey has been at times most methodical, as in the work of Sister M. F. Zeller.[2]

But obviously the formal attractiveness of a maxim cannot be separated from its meaning. A maxim like:

La fin du bien est un mal; la fin du mal est un bien. (M.P., 14)

may to begin with offer a pleasurable symmetry but, as J. Truchet rightly notes, we are strongly tempted to reject it as a disappointing truism.[3] For all its tantalising neatness, the shell is empty, or else what it contained has evaporated.

One of the best approaches to an assessment of the artistic merit of the *Maximes* and to the individual talent of its author is to relate certain recurring patterns to certain basic preoccupations of La Rochefoucauld. This is, for instance, what C. Rosso did with precision and elegance when studying the dialectics of compensation in the *Maximes* from the point of view of both ideological content and stylistic forms.[4]

In the preceding chapters I have inevitably touched upon some problems of style which now deserve some further comments. The ambiguity of certain words raises a question of esthetics. To what extent was such ambiguity an advantage

---

[1] Op. cit., pp. 87–90.   [2] See above, p. 7.
[3] Introduction, p. 1.
[4] 'Démarches et structures de compensation dans les "Maximes" de La Rochefoucauld', communication au XVIIe Congrès de l'Association Internationale des Etudes Françaises, published in the *Cahiers* of the Association, No. 18, March, 1966, pp. 114–24.

or a disadvantage to La Rochefoucauld as an artist? There are other similar questions I am tempted to ask which are very much in the line of this present study. As C. Rosso so successfully proved, appreciation of style entails a certain amount of selection and the choice of a focus. My own considerations on the esthetic value of the *Maximes* spring from a feeling of uneasiness and from the suspicion that, at times, we praise La Rochefoucauld for the wrong reasons, either because we are strongly influenced by our modern ideas on literature or because we cling to accepted views on French classicism which, I think, should be queried. I have already questioned the eulogistic assertion that La Rochefoucauld is remarkable for his use of the 'mot juste'; and this is not the only point where a reader's personal analysis might conflict with traditional views.

The maxim, it is well known, was a fashionable genre. Its merits rested on a long tradition. Its brevity was attractive, the more so as it was a difficulty. There was in the mind of the cultivated Frenchman a hankering after the kind of conciseness that only Latin, it seems, could achieve. The maxim therefore presupposed nimbleness in the use of words, even wit. Moreover it had always appeared to be the right vehicle for moral judgements or the expression of general truths about mankind.

In a way the genre suited La Rochefoucauld's investigations into the field of psychology and ethics. The brevity, pungency and self-sufficiency of the individual maxim corresponded to the sharp individual sounding at a given level of experience. On the other hand there were a great many disadavantages. The maxim carried with it the rather stale flavour of having too many times stated the obvious, even if the obvious was a respectable commonplace. It had too often been used for heavy moralising or for practical advice in keeping with a worldly wisdom which left no room for discovery. The delicate probing into man's heart was something altogether different.

The rigidity of the form – how often had the maxim been flatteringly compared to unyielding materials such as pearls, gems or precious metals? – did not fit very well the fluctuating nature of the complex feelings or mental attitudes La Rochefoucauld was trying to convey.

To be successful a maxim, as used by La Rochefoucauld, must be the reverse of a commonplace; it must provoke a shock, embody a discovery, and also make the discovery convincing. All this implied a careful handling of the tools the moralist had at his disposal.

The most obvious technique to shock is to use the paradox, which, by definition, goes against accepted opinions. It can be done very simply by reversing the terms of an existing aphorism. La Rochefoucauld resorts to various rhetorical patterns, among which is antithesis. But by itself antithesis is not a very good tool to provoke a shock, as it corresponds to our mental habits (we automatically think in antithetical terms – black: white, day: night, good: bad, etc.) and we accept it too readily. It has therefore to be presented in a special way to produce its effect.

Let us start with a comparatively simple illustration:

Il est difficile de comprendre combien est grande la ressemblance et la différence qu'il y a entre tous les hommes. (M.P., 19)

The force of the maxim lies in the coupling right in the middle of the sentence of the two opposite words 'ressemblance', 'différence'; this is not just stating that men are, paradoxically, both alike and different; the statement is considerably modified and reinforced by the opening words stressing the difficulty anyone (the writer, the reader) has in appreciating the degree of either 'ressemblance' or 'différence' between men, so that an element of wonder, even of puzzlement is introduced into the maxim.

Nor need the use of antithesis result in a negative statement:

La constance en amour est une inconstance perpétuelle... (175)

This is in a way a simple antithesis, the simpler, and the more absolute, in that 'constance' and 'inconstance' have the same root; this might just lead to the mere destruction of the value of constancy, the two terms cancelling each other out. But this first antithesis is checked by a second one, the operative word 'perpétuelle' standing for continuity and being attached not to 'constance' but to 'inconstance'. A new positive order emerges, suggesting, in endless succession, the miracle of falling in love over and over again with the same person.

The art with which La Rochefoucauld can play with antithesis without producing a crude and sweeping statement can be very fine. Here is for instance the most exquisite poise:

La simplicité affectée est une imposture délicate. (289)

The four operative words stand in unexpected relations of coupling and opposition. The maxim is not a blunt statement that an open countenance and unassuming manner may be nothing but a mask hiding conceit and vanity. What La Rochefoucauld does here is to assess as accurately as possible the value of a certain attitude prompted by our *amour-propre*. It is a mixed value which calls for the most intricate pattern. The words 'simplicité' and 'affectée' clash, for we usually think of simplicity as the opposite of affectation. So do the words 'imposture' and 'délicate', a strange alliance of strong disapproval and gentle praise. At the same time the four words are closely related since 'affectée' and 'imposture' both imply deceit while 'simplicité' and 'délicate' both relate to worthwhile qualities. This complicated interaction of the words upon one another results in a strict control over the pleasant or unpleasant harmonics of each term. We are left only with nuances. Any definite moral judgement is suspended and, through a very sophisticated use of paradox, we have been made to appreciate a singularly sophisticated attitude in which charm nicely balances – almost justifies – its basic artfulness.

Because patterns like symmetry or antithesis are too easily accepted by our minds, the art of La Rochefoucauld consists at times in using a symmetrical pattern to express what one could call an 'asymmetrical' relation and, by doing so, in producing an unexpected effect and compelling us to discard our automatic reactions. But habits of mind are very tenacious and in some cases readers have missed the point of the 'asymmetry'.

A maxim like:

La bonne grâce est au corps ce que le bon sens est à l'esprit. (67)

worried many commentators, both in the seventeenth century and later.[1] What they thought should correspond to 'la bonne grâce du corps' was something like 'la délicatesse de l'esprit'. It was even suggested, in order to justify La Rochefoucauld, that, at the time he wrote, the connotation of 'bon sens' was sufficiently elastic to include 'délicatesse de l'esprit'. All this is wrong, I think. The whole impact of the maxim depends precisely in not being given the expected quality, so as to create a new parallel between the grace of the body – natural harmony and economy of movements – and 'bon sens' (in its cartesian connotation) – the natural and straightforward working of our intellect.

Some of the most successful maxims are perhaps those in which La Rochefoucauld does away altogether with the characteristic of rigidity which seems inherent in the genre:

Quand on aime, on doute souvent de ce qu'on croit le plus. (348)

The antithesis between 'doute' and 'croit' is partly modified and enriched by the addition of 'souvent' (frequency of doubt) and 'le plus' (fervour of belief). The paradoxical statement of the self-contradictory nature of our judgement when we are in love assumes here a particular quality of fluidity as soon as we try to clarify the meaning of the maxim. Does it mean that what our heart wants so fervently to believe our reason doubts or, on the contrary, that when our reason reassures us strongly our anxious heart is ready to doubt? Both meanings are acceptable; in the never-ending dialogue between heart and reason the parts are constantly reversed.

This is the kind of ambiguity which is artistically successful. It does not confuse the issue nor tempt us to look uneasily for another level of experience to which the maxim might more

[1] For these various comments see the footnote of J. Truchet and also the note of L. Martin-Chauffier in the Pléiade edition (op. cit., pp. 635–6).

rightly refer. It remains within the paradox of the self-divided lover but gives to the pattern of this paradox a dynamic quality which translates admirably the oscillations of hope and fear in the lover's mind.

We have already met a great deal of ambiguity of a different type in the *Maximes* when we hesitated about the particular connotation La Rochefoucauld had chosen to give to a word in a given maxim. In some cases it results in enriching the maxim with a second meaning,[1] whether La Rochefoucauld intended it or not. Very often it is an interesting pointer to the extreme complexity of the author's views. But it also reveals the inadequacy of vocabulary which he cannot always overcome. This is where the difficulties I mentioned in the first chapter[2] are most apparent. Our hesitations as to the exact meaning of some of the maxims may and do in fact stimulate our mind but, from an artistic point of view, this ambiguity is certainly an imperfection.

I do not think anyhow that La Rochefoucauld intended to stimulate the minds of his readers in this particular way. As a rule he tries to pinpoint with the greatest possible degree of precision the attitude he analyses and takes care not to go beyond the evidence:

L'aversion du mensonge est souvent une imperceptible ambition de rendre nos témoignages considérables, et d'attirer à nos paroles un respect de religion. (63)

The key word is 'imperceptible'. It may be that our loathing for lies springs from our desire to see other people developing an almost religious respect for what we say. This kind of motivation is such that neither the others nor ourselves are aware of it, so that there is in fact a certain amount of genuine frankness in some people, at least very near the surface. The whole point of this 'imperceptible', which stands in such a forceful contrast with the ponderous and solemn second half of the sentence, is to assess with some precision at what depth of consciousness the motivation lies.

[1] See particularly maxim 206 analysed on p. 73.　　[2] See above, pp. 9–12.

Modern taste does not willingly accept the basically self-contained nature of La Rochefoucauld's maxims. We are encouraged by almost two centuries of romantic literature to measure the achievement of a text by the amount of suggestions it radiates. Therefore the compactness of the *Maximes* is praised as going inevitably with the power of expanding. W. G. Moore remarked that Nietzsche particularly admired in the *Maximes* 'the paradoxical blend of brevity in actual expression and wide range of meaning and suggestion'.[1]

The paradox is easily accepted. Whenever we face the characteristics of abstractness and compression in a seventeenth-century writer, Gide's well-known definition of classicism leaps to mind: 'L'art d'exprimer le plus en disant le moins.' Indeed a number of people think of La Rochefoucauld's maxims as some kind of small tablets which once placed in the right medium, would naturally expand or be like those Japanese toys mentioned by Proust which, no bigger than tiny bits of paper, unfold when put in water and reveal the wealth of shapes and colours contained in them.

I have increasing doubts about the cogency of Gide's famous definition. It certainly does not apply to La Fontaine whose art lies essentially in checking the power of association of the words he uses. Nor does it account for Racine's strictly functional handling of conventional diction. I would even be tempted to suggest that the art of the classicist lies in controlling the tendency to expansion of abstract nouns and multivalent expressions. If Bossuet managed to produce a strong effect with the supremely vague expression 'un jeu ne sais quoi' it is in fact because the connotation of this 'je ne sais quoi' is carefully defined by the context:

Notre corps prend un autre nom; même celui de cadavre, dit Tertullien, parce qu'il nous montre encore quelque forme humaine, ne lui demeure pas longtemps; il devient un je ne sais quoi, qui n'a plus de nom dans aucune langue; tant il est vrai que tout meurt en lui, jusqu'à ces termes funèbres par lesquels on exprimait ses malheureux restes! (*Oraison funèbre de Henriette-Anne d'Angleterre*)

[1] Op. cit., p. 83.

The physical revulsion in front of death is raised here to the intellectual level (intellectual horror being perhaps the worst horror of all): the impossibility of finding a word, a name for what is left of us. The 'je ne sais quoi' is brought back to its literal meaning and thus translates with terrifying precision the complete impotence of the mind.

In the case of La Rochefoucauld I very much doubt whether the art of condensation is meant to 'exprimer le plus'. He took great care never to express more than the evidence.[1] The effect produced on the mind of the reader is not, I think, to stimulate his thoughts in all sorts of directions but to focus his attention onto a carefully circumscribed area.

In this respect La Rochefoucauld's use of metaphors is illuminating. They are, as a rule, unobtrusive, deliberately chosen among commonplace images, traditionally accepted. Virtues are lost in self-interest like rivers in the sea. Fire, wind, water, plants, glass are used in turn, sparingly and never as a picturesque conceit. There is no danger of our attention being transferred to something exciting but extraneous. We appreciate the aptness of the metaphor chosen, not its intrinsic beauty.

The aptness may result in something so revealing that the effect of a comparison may give us a shock:

Le soleil ni la mort ne se peuvent regarder fixement. (26)

The concrete value of the word 'soleil' is immediately pushed aside, as soon as the word has fulfilled its function, that is to make us realise that we cannot stare at death.

Although unobtrusive, these images are carefully chosen and are very much related to La Rochefoucauld's exploratory study of human nature. We remember how he saw man as a prisoner of time, carried along through a process of evolution; how man, for him, is conditioned by his *forme maîtresse* and

---

[1] This would also explain why he added such restrictive expressions as 'le plus souvent', 'souvent', 'quelquefois'. These additions are often ascribed to a wish, on his part, to spare his readers' feelings and to soften the blow – an explanation which, it seems to me, does not fit with either La Rochefoucauld's intellectual integrity, or his esthetic preoccupations.

also by a kind of dynamic pattern. The laws which condition him in this way are very similar to the laws of nature which rule the properties and growth of the vegetable kingdom. It is therefore not surprising that La Rochefoucauld seems to have a special liking for images borrowed from plants:

Le mérite des hommes a sa saison aussi bien que les fruits. (291)

Chaque talent dans les hommes, de même que chaque arbre, a ses propriétés et ses effets qui lui sont tous particuliers. (M.S., 25)

La plupart des hommes ont comme les plantes des propriétés cachées que le hasard fait découvrir. (344)

La grâce de la nouveauté est à l'amour ce que la fleur est sur les fruits... (274)

The art of integrating the metaphor in the thought expressed so that it becomes entirely absorbed in it results at times in the type of image which ceases to be an image:

La jeunesse est une ivresse continuelle: c'est la fièvre de la raison. (271)

La plus juste comparaison qu'on puisse faire de l'amour, c'est celle de la fièvre... (M.S., 59)

Is this in fact a comparison? We are told by La Rochefoucauld that our passions, like all our psychological reactions, are conditioned by the state of our body. Perhaps love is not only like a fever: it is a fever. The 'fièvre de la raison' which characterises youth may be more than metaphorical; it may express a physiological state in which the brain reacts more quickly and also more extravagantly.

It seems therefore that La Rochefoucauld has set strict limitations to the power of suggestion in the *Maximes*. Their compactness is not a mere formal quality. We cannot take anything from a maxim, nor can we add anything to it.

Endeavours to take a maxim as the starting point for a little story (it has been tried)[1] or to equate it with a detail taken from

---

[1] By Jacques de Lacretelle, in *Tableau de la Littérature Française*, Gallimard, 1939, pp. 37–40.

the author's life (as some commentators have done) show a complete misunderstanding of the work and are poor responses to the text.

Of course, as we get more experience of life, of men and of ourselves, a greater number of maxims become connected with more and more personal concrete experiences which are for each of us precious illustrations of the truth of the book. But even when we have reached the stage when La Rochefoucauld's *Maximes* are for us like a rich picture book full of associations with our own life, we know very well that we have not added anything or modified anything. The gap between our own experience, however rich, and the maxim cannot be bridged. The maxim has not expanded. La Rochefoucauld has cut off his maxim from his personal experience as well as from that of his future readers, except as far as its truth is concerned. Here rests the triumph of art and its paradoxical quality.

Le soleil ni la mort ne se peuvent regarder fixement.

This is perfect communication, reality forced on our consciousness and acknowledged by us (if not today, at least tomorrow) with a shock of illumination. At the same time the artistic achievement of this maxim makes it self-sufficient, belonging to a world of its own, so that it can never become stale and retains its power of appearing new and striking each time. This is the same kind of Phœnix-like quality which, according to Valéry, a beautiful line of poetry possesses.

VARIATIONS ON A THEME

La Rochefoucauld's longer maxims and the *Réflexions Diverses* have stylistic features of their own, but are perhaps not so different from the epigrammatic form of the maxim as one might expect.

The first of the *Maximes Supprimées*, the picture of *amour-propre*, achieves a kind of perfection which never fails to attract the reader and is probably the best illustration of what the author can do with more room available for stylistic manipulations:

L'amour-propre est l'amour de soi-même, et de toutes choses pour soi; il rend les hommes idolâtres d'eux-mêmes, et les rendrait les tyrans des autres si la fortune leur en donnait les moyens; il ne se repose jamais hors de soi, et ne s'arrête dans les sujets étrangers que comme les abeilles sur les fleurs, pour en tirer ce qui lui est propre. Rien n'est si impétueux que ses désirs, rien de si caché que ses desseins, rien de si habile que ses conduites; ses souplesses ne se peuvent représenter, ses transformations passent celles des métamorphoses, et ses raffinements ceux de la chimie. On ne peut sonder la profondeur, ni percer les ténèbres de ses abîmes. Là il est à couvert des yeux les plus pénétrants; il y fait mille insensibles tours et retours. Là il est souvent invisible à lui-même, il y conçoit, il y nourrit, et il y élève, sans le savoir, un grand nombre d'affections et de haines; il en forme de si monstrueuses que, lorsqu'il les a mises au jour, il les méconnaît, ou il ne peut se résoudre à les avouer. De cette nuit qui le couvre naissent les ridicules persuasions qu'il a de lui-même; de là viennent ses erreurs, ses ignorances, ses grossièretés et ses niaiseries sur son sujet; de là vient qu'il croit que ses sentiments sont morts lorsqu'ils ne sont qu'endormis, qu'il s'imagine n'avoir plus envie de courir dès qu'il se repose, et qu'il pense avoir perdu tous les goûts qu'il a rassasiés. Mais cette obscurité épaisse, qui le cache à lui-même, n'empêche pas qu'il ne voie parfaitement ce qui est hors de lui, en quoi il est semblable à nos yeux, qui découvrent tout, et sont aveugles seulement pour eux-mêmes. En effet dans ses plus grands intérêts, et dans ses plus importantes affaires, où la violence de ses souhaits appelle toute son attention, il voit, il sent, il entend, il imagine, il soupçonne, il pénètre, il devine tout; de sorte qu'on est tenté de croire que chacune de ses passions a une espèce de magie qui lui est propre. Rien n'est si intime et si fort que ses attachements, qu'il essaye de rompre inutilement à la vue des malheurs extrêmes qui le menacent. Cependant il fait quelquefois en peu de temps, et sans aucun effort, ce qu'il n'a pu faire avec tous ceux dont il est capable dans le cours de plusieurs années; d'où l'on pourrait conclure assez vraisemblablement que c'est par lui-même que ses désirs sont allumés, plutôt que par la beauté et par le mérite de ses objets; que son goût est le prix qui les relève, et le fard qui les embellit; que c'est après lui-même qu'il court, et qu'il suit son gré, lorsqu'il suit les choses qui sont à son gré. Il est tous les contraires; il est impérieux et obéissant, sincère et dissimulé, miséricordieux et cruel, timide et audacieux. Il a de différentes inclinations selon la diversité des tempéraments qui le tournent, et le dévouent tantôt à la gloire, tantôt aux richesses, et tantôt aux plaisirs; il en change selon le changement de nos âges, de nos fortunes et de nos expériences; mais il lui est indifférent d'en avoir plusieurs ou de n'en avoir qu'une, parce qu'il se partage en plusieurs et se ramasse en une quand il le faut, et comme il lui plaît. Il est inconstant, et outre les changements qui viennent des causes étrangères, il y en a une infinité qui naissent de lui, et de son propre fonds; il est inconstant d'inconstance, de légereté, d'amour, de nouveauté, de lassitude et de dégôut; il est capricieux, et on le voit quelquefois travailler avec le dernier empressement, et avec des travaux incroyables, à obtenir des choses qui ne lui sont point avantageuses, et qui même lui sont nuisibles, mais qu'il poursuit parce qu'il les veut. Il est bizarre, et met souvent toute son application dans les emplois les plus frivoles; il trouve tout son plaisir dans les plus fades, et conserve toute sa fierté dans les plus méprisables. Il est dans tous les états de la vie, et dans toutes les conditions; il vit partout, et il vit de tout, il vit de rien; il s'accommode des choses, et de leur privation; il passe même dans le parti des gens qui lui font la guerre, il entre dans leurs desseins; et ce qui est admirable, il se hait lui-même avec eux, il conjure sa perte, il travaille même à sa ruine. Enfin il ne se soucie que d'être, et pourvu qu'il soit, il veut bien être son ennemi. Il ne faut donc pas s'étonner s'il se joint quelquefois à la plus rude austérité, et s'il entre si hardiment en société avec elle pour se détruire, parce que, dans le même temps qu'il se ruine en un endroit, il se rétablit en un autre; quand on pense qu'il quitte son plaisir, il ne fait que le suspendre, ou le changer, et lors même qu'il est vaincu et qu'on croit en être défait, on le retrouve qui triomphe dans sa propre défaite. Voilà la peinture de l'amour-propre, dont toute la vie n'est qu'une grande et longue agitation; la mer en est une image sensible, et l'amour-propre trouve dans le flux et le reflux de ses vagues continuelles une fidèle expression de la succession turbulente de ses pensées, et de ses éternels mouvements.

We have moved now from the compactness of the maxim to what seems to be the deliberate expansion of one of La Rochefoucauld's basic themes: the all-embracing nature of self-love. It is obviously a set piece meant to stand by itself with the hallmark of impeccable finish. It was in fact first published by itself.[1]

Despite the magnificent enlargement of the final sentence which suggests infinity in space and time through its image, diction and rhythm, the structure of the piece is a close one, like that of a theorem: definition ('L'amour-propre est l'amour de soi-même et de toutes choses pour soi') – demonstration – conclusion ('Voilà la peinture de l'amour-propre...'). Within this simple framework the pattern of the composition is far from simple. One could say roughly that it is made up of a series of tentative approaches to corner an elusive object – the essence of self-love – each movement of the pursuer ('On serait tenté de croire...', 'Quand on pense que...') being baulked, each qualification destined to encircle *amour-propre* being negated by a label pointing in the opposite direction ('impérieux et obéissant, sincère et dissimulé...'). The general impression is of a frustrating search inside a maze where sinuous paths lead to a dead end or repeatedly bring one back to the centre of the labyrinth until it is fully realised that this centre is the very negation of the search: 'Enfin il ne se soucie que d'être...', the point where essence fuses with existence and thus escapes for ever.

Yet it is not the image of the labyrinth La Rochefoucauld has chosen but that of the sea ('La mer en est une image sensible...'). Undoubtedly nothing can better render the cease-less agitation of self-love, its constant movement forward and backward and even the gratuitousness of that dynamism. However, this image, which provides a beautiful ending, does not really account retrospectively for the pattern of the passage. There is no dominant image. The bee appears flittingly, chemistry is mentioned, *fard* brings a brief touch of artificial prettiness. The author has used the resources of imagery very sparingly. He relies much more on the kind of semi-figurative expressions in which the original concrete import has been rubbed down by usage so that it has very little evocative relief ('percer les ténèbres', 'sonder la profondeur', 'ses désirs sont

---

[1] It was published anonymously in a collection of little essays by different hands. It was withdrawn by La Rochefoucauld in the second edition of the *Maximes*, and reappeared in the posthumous edition of 1693. (Cf. J. Truchet's notice, p. 133.)

allumés', etc.). These play an essential part and constitute a link between the generally abstract vocabulary of the passage and the concrete impression of perpetual movement and resilient liveliness.

Moreover the image of the sea would not be sufficient to describe accurately the fickle nature of self-love. In spite of the ocean's turbulence, there is in the ebb and flow of the waves and of the tide an element of regularity and of predictability, a reassuring binary rhythm which self-love assumes only occasionally when its self-contradictory manifestations are given in the form of a straightforward antithesis ('il vit de tout, il vit de rien'). The main point about the behaviour of *amour-propre* is that it is unpredictable and essentially mysterious. This puzzling characteristic is stated several times with reference to magic ('chacune de ses passions a une espèce de magie'), unaccountable quaintness ('il est bizarre'), even alchemy perhaps ('les raffinements...de la chimie').

Much of the effect of irregular movement is given by the extreme variety in the form and length of the sentences and by the modifications in rhythm. For instance a ternary pattern may unfold at a sedate pace ('Rien n'est si impétueux que ses désirs, rien de si caché que ses desseins, rien de si habile que ses conduites...', repeated as a pattern in the following sentence) or on the contrary suggest rapid shifts of direction ('et le dévouent tantôt à la gloire, tantôt aux richesses et tantôt aux plaisirs...'). The comparatively static impression produced by the long sentence expressing the paradox of the eye which can see everything except itself is replaced in the next sentence by a quick acceleration of rhythm ('il voit, il sent, il entend, il imagine, il soupçonne, il pénètre, il devine tout'). The basic restlessness of self-love is thus forced upon the reader who is never lulled into passivity or compliance by the recurrence of a dominant rhythm. At the same time there is no unpleasant jerkiness. Sentences are connected by almost invisible threads. Thus the idea of the obscurity hiding self-love is followed up for a time to introduce new points ('De cette nuit qui le couvre...', 'Mais cette obscurité qui le couvre...').

Elsewhere we find a gradual movement up the scale of inter-connected adjectives (*inconstant* leading to *capricieux*, the latter leading to *bizarre*). Conjunctions so useful in providing strong articulations in a logical argument, such as *mais, cepen-dant, d'où* etc. are very few, and there is but a faint trace of rhetorical devices ('Là il est à couvert...', 'Là il est souvent ...'). In fact the fluidity in the movement of the whole passage seems to imitate the 'mille insensibles tours et retours' of self-love itself.

Perhaps the most remarkable stylistic feature is the obsessive repetition of the pronoun *il*. Here we come to the central idea in this picture of self-love, that of metamorphosis ('ses transformations passent celles des métamorphoses') admir-ably underlined by the protean nature of this *il*. Concrete presence or abstract entity? Animal? Vegetable? Mineral (as 'les raffinements...de la chimie' would suggest)? He or it? Each of its states is so evanescent that no clear definition is possible. It seems at times to be personified and endowed with activities and feelings which are specifically those of human beings: loving and hating, pursuing glory or wealth, using imagination, capable of austerity. But it is also given as a sort of undefined animal, at times a monster of the depths whose constant twists and turns are heavily screened by some liquid opacity. Whatever the medium through which it moves, it possesses the basic properties of the living organism which men and animals share: reproduction, feeding one's young and oneself ('il conçoit, nourrit, élève...', 'une infinité qui naissent de lui...', 'les goûts qu'il a rassasiés...', 'il vit de tout...'), the use of senses ('il voit, il sent, il entend') and of course motion.

This living organism is at times reduced to a single organ: the eye; or even appears as the most primitive form of life, the most enduring too. The sentence:

Mais il lui est indifférent d'en avoir plusieurs ou de n'en avoir qu'une [inclination], parce qu'il se partage en plusieurs et se ramasse en une...

suggests to us some of the strange biological properties of the amoeba. It is only a passing suggestion. We are immediately brought back to the intellectual features of self-love through the mention of abstract qualities.

Everywhere in the passage abstract nouns counterbalance the verbs of movement. In fact the general characteristic of abstractness in the diction provides admirably for the constant metamorphoses; it operates a tight control over associations of ideas. The *il* remains invisible to our imagination. Nor are its multiple activities ever particularised; vague words like *choses, conditions, desseins, objets, emplois,* etc. cover the whole field of human endeavours and circumstances without mentioning a single one. So vast and general is the picture that when we come to the climactic 'Il vit partout, et il vit de tout, il vit de rien' those very large abstractions *partout, tout, rien* stand out with all their potential vigour released and affix the seal of the absolute on what we already know of *amour-propre's* ubiquity and paradoxical resilience.

Basically the art of La Rochefoucauld in this passage is not very different from his art in the short maxims. We find the same compactness, the same limitations deliberately imposed on the evocative powers of words, in order to suppress any freak associations while at the same time giving to those same words their full impact.

Nowhere has La Rochefoucauld expressed more forcibly the fundamental truth that the all-pervading presence of self-love is not a theory, but a biological fact. But the passage is not the expansion of a theme; it is a richly compressed summary of many of the features of self-love to be found elsewhere in his work. The word 'variations' that I chose as a heading for this analysis may be misleading, may suggest superfluous embroideries. As it is, the variations in rhythm are strictly functional. The length of the passage has enabled La Rochefoucauld to make the most of the qualities of fluidity and dynamism which, as we have seen, are also present in some of his maxims, and to give with an admirable effect of immediacy a picture of *amour-propre,* so to speak, in action.

My study of La Rochefoucauld ends deliberately with this glance at the obscure depths where his most daring explorations have taken him. A clear summary of all that constitutes the outstanding value of his work is what I cannot yet attempt. As far as I am concerned, there are still too many unanswered questions raised by the text.

Perhaps the most persistent impression I retain after each re-reading of the *Maximes* and of the *Réflexions* is that of a grim and lonely quest for the true nature of man. This is no doubt what all moralists intend. But none of them, I think, has pursued his search with such relentless application nor has acknowledged his frustration and maybe ultimate defeat so pitilessly.

LA BRUYÈRE

5

THE ECCENTRIC MORALIST

La Bruyère may appear easier to appreciate than La Roche-foucauld because some of the facets of his work make a direct appeal to our heart or to our sense of humour. It is nevertheless very difficult to come to a definite judgement of value on the *Caractères* taken as a whole. Our own century is particularly hesitant, and this hesitation to commit ourselves to a definite appraisal of the book tends to keep La Bruyère in a respectable but rather dull place by-passed by the great movements of revaluation. Julian Benda's attack[1] – unfair and illuminating at the same time – failed to dislodge La Bruyère from his too-secure niche in a dead end or to bring him nearer to us, for better or for worse. Roland Barthes speaks of the *malaise* of the modern reader confronted in the *Caractères* with a picture of the world which is both familiar and alien.[2] One of the most recent studies, *Les Caractères de La Bruyère, bible de l'honnête homme*, by André Stegman[3] seems in its sub-title to confirm the traditional image of innocuous respectability, but, after a remarkably thorough analysis of the work, the author ends on a non-committal note, and chooses as a final quali-fication of the book the ambiguous adjective *singulier*: original? strange? or a mixture of both?

There is a fascinating quality about the work which even the most tepid admirers acknowledge and try to sum up by saying that whatever reservations they may have about La Bruyère he was one of the greatest 'stylists'. This concern for 'style', for the problems facing the writer, is undoubtedly an impor-tant aspect of the *Caractères*. But to call La Bruyère a stylist is not, in itself, a satisfactory explanation. Style does not exist in a vacuum. A certain way of saying things corresponds to

[1] This provoking essay was published in *Tableau de la Littérature Française*, op. cit.
[2] *La Bruyère: Les Caractères* précédé de 'La Bruyère, du Mythe à l'Ecriture', Roland Barthes, Union Générale d'Editions, Paris, 1963.
[3] Larousse, Paris, 1972.

a certain way of seeing them, and the fascinating quality of La Bruyère's writing may well reside in the way – or ways – he chose to look at men and at life: the curious angles of vision, the parcelling out of topics, the unexpected and puzzling shifting of the camera, from the close-up to the panoramic scene, from earth to heaven.

I say puzzling, and some would add irritatingly so; for the almost universal reproach directed against Les Caractères has been the apparent untidiness of the work, its lack of unity, its lack of pattern.

A great variety of subjects is grouped somewhat loosely under a number of headings: 'Du Mérite Personnel', 'De la Cour', 'De l'Homme', and so on, and the observations made by the author do not always have an obvious link with the heading. In the course of the various editions La Bruyère moved some paragraphs from one section to another without the reason for the move being very clear in some cases.

The form adopted by the writer varies from the epigrammatic maxim to the short story, such as the tale of Emire at the end of the chapter 'Des Femmes'. Even if we think of the portrait as being La Bruyère's most typical form of expression, it is difficult at times to decide what is a portrait and what is not. La Bruyère may be concerned with a particular individual to whom he gives a name; such is the portrait of Straton ('De la Cour', 96) which stresses very individual characteristics. But a name may equally apply to a type of man, to the allegory of a vice (Gnathon, the glutton).

Very often there is no name attached to the portrait: 'le courtisan', 'le financier'. Even the precarious individualisation given by the definite article tends to vanish: 'un homme de mérite', 'un bel esprit', 'une femme de la ville'. More than once what is portrayed is not one man but a group of men: 'les grands', 'le peuple'. The dividing line between the portrait and the general remark is not clear-cut. A paragraph may start with a portrait which becomes by almost imperceptible degrees an abstract statement about mankind, or the other way round.

Moreover, and this is perhaps more upsetting, there is no

real coherence of thought in the book. Critics have had a happy time collecting the contradictions they have found in the course of their reading.[1] Was La Bruyère aware of these inconsistencies? In the fifth edition of the *Caractères*, after noting how a man's good qualities are seen as bad ones as soon as he falls out of favour, the passage ends rather abruptly with the following paragraph:

Je me contredis, il est vrai: accusez-en les hommes, dont je ne fais que rapporter les jugements; je ne dis pas de différents hommes, je dis les mêmes, qui jugent si différemment. (Des Jugements, 93)

It is not very clear whether this remark is aimed at public opinion, the vagaries of which he has just stressed, or whether he includes himself among the men he criticises.

Should one suppose that the conflicting opinions expressed by La Bruyère are to be cancelled out by a unifying process, by the intention, on the part of the author, to give a definite shape to the succession of his 'caractères de ce siècle' and to the order of the chapters? La Bruyère hinted at a *plan d'ensemble* in one of his prefaces to the book and was even more specific in the Preface to his 'Discours de Réception à l'Académie Française' where he states that the first fifteen chapters of the *Caractères* are destined to make man realise his vices and follies and to lead to the sixteenth chapter where atheism is attacked and the Christian ideal offered as the wisest attitude. As Robert Garapon remarks, this borrowing of Pascal's plan for his apology is very much an afterthought used for self-justification.[2]

A few critics have, however, tried to discover a coherent pattern in the book and none with such care, patience and finesse as André Stegman,[3] who has examined more particularly La Bruyère's remodelling of his work in order to achieve a more satisfactory grouping and progression of topics. His demonstration is attractively presented. But one is perhaps more tempted to admire the critic's own remodelling of the

---

[1] Particularly Julien Benda in his notes on the *Caractères* in his edition of La Bruyère (*Oeuvres Complètes de la Bruyère*, Paris, N.R.F., 1951).
[2] 'Introduction', p. xxiv.   [3] Op. cit., pp. 29–72.

Caractères into a complex architecture than to be altogether convinced by his arguments.

Whatever La Bruyère's assertions and his attempts to give more unity to his work, our doubt persists. The best way to look at the book, as far as its overall shape is concerned, may be, I think, to consider it as a kind of diary which spread over twenty years of the author's life and where he noted at different times in different ways the different topics which interested him at a given moment.

Besides, trying to find a close structure for the *Caractères* is perhaps the wrong approach. To look for some kind of 'architecture' which would give the work a harmonious form is to look for something uncompromisingly static, and it can be argued that La Bruyère does not anyhow need such a justification.

The lack of unity, the variety of subjects treated (literary criticism, fashions, politics, metaphysical problems, psychology of children) need not be explained away as the apparently negative features of an untidy literary work. They have a positive significance and can help us to see what kind of a moralist La Bruyère is.

An important part of his book is certainly inspired by the moralist's purpose, which is to study man within the limitations of nature and reason. A fair number of remarks, of maxims, even, remind us of La Rochefoucauld, and we find there the same clear insight into the human condition and into the working of the human mind. But, if we had a slight hesitation in using the term moralist in its strict connotation in the case of La Rochefoucauld, when we come to La Bruyère it is obvious that the author of the *Caractères* does not confine himself to the carefully circumscribed universe of the moralist. Something seems to happen to that near perfect sphere which was the world of La Fontaine, La Rochefoucauld, Racine or Madame de Lafayette. The centre tends to shift away from its formerly stable position; under the pressure of those eccentric impulses the sphere bursts and La Bruyère's investigations shoot out in all directions in a kind of centrifugal movement.

This may be viewed as a historical phenomenon. La Bruyère was thirty years younger than La Rochefoucauld, and the *Caractères* may be considered, and have been considered,[1] as marking the beginning of the disintegration of French classicism. But it may equally well be a personal choice, the product of an original mind, of a restless intelligence impatient with limitations, ambitious and passionately inquisitive. The two explanations are not mutually exclusive.

I would venture to say that the most interesting aspects of the work – and some of its shortcomings too – are highly significant of this 'explosion' of the moralist's universe.

CHRISTIAN OUTLOOK

Beyond the world of nature

The fact that La Rochefoucauld's *Maximes* were probably written against a background of a Christian tradition and contemporary religious preoccupations may give a somewhat ambiguous colouring to the word 'moralist' and affect at times his terminology. However he took great care to remove the maxims which had some religious import. In so doing he fell into line with the other classicists who, whatever their own personal beliefs and traditional Christian background, limited their study of man and society to what man, with the help of his human reason only, could know of his human condition on earth. They left religion to the theologians and philosophy to the philosophers.

Was the co-existence of two different outlooks on man a consequence of a split in European sensibility created by the crisis of the Late Renaissance, as has been suggested? There may have been other causes as well. But undeniably the 'two-truth world' which was to be denounced vigorously at the end of the nineteenth century and in the twentieth century[2] is nowhere so much in evidence as in French classicism. Works

---

[1] This emerges clearly from Julien Benda's essay, and he sees La Bruyère as a forerunner of modern decadence (see particularly the conclusion of the essay, op. cit., p. 186).

[2] One thinks of Péguy whose poetry reflects the wholeness of a catholic universe, of neo-scholasticism, of thinkers like Teilhard de Chardin, etc. – and also of such a book as Kathleen Nott's *The Emperor's Clothes*.

like La Fontaine's *Fables*, Madame de Lafayette's *Princesse de Clèves*, La Rochefoucauld's *Maximes*, even Racine's tragedies, show the kind of truth these writers were concerned with, and how they kept within the limitations of the moralist's universe. Conversely, even if Pascal made use of some of Montaigne's views on the human condition, his single purpose was evidently to reject the world of nature and reason and to replace it by the world of faith. Bossuet might at times vie with the moralists in psychological insight[1] but stated uncompromisingly that all earthly values are meaningless *sub specie aeternitatis*. There may have been clashes between two such contradictory truths. They are not discernible in the major works of the period. We have the impression that the man of the times found it comparatively easy, and certainly convenient, to live parallel lives on two different levels. Louis XIV would respectfully listen to one of Bossuet's *Oraisons Funèbres* telling him that all the things that mattered to him were nothing but vanity and dust, and in the evening enjoy a play by Racine or Molière, a form of entertainment which the same Bossuet firmly denounced as incompatible with a Christian life.

La Bruyère, however, although a moralist, does not abide by the rules of peaceful co-existence, by this kind of gentleman's agreement which established a clear-cut division between the world of nature and reason and the world of faith.

His concern for the teaching of the Gospels moves him to devote a chapter of his book ('De la Chaire') to a criticism of contemporary preaching and to an impassioned plea for the kind of sermon which would fulfil its basic religious purpose. And, as we know, his most obvious attempt at an incursion into the field of metaphysics and apologetics is the final section of the *Caractères* ('Des Esprits Forts') which is an attack against atheists and a sustained effort to prove the existence of God by using arguments borrowed from Pascal and Descartes.

We might be tempted to consider the last two chapters of

---

[1] This fine analytical power is perhaps at its best in the first sections of his *Maximes et Réflexions sur la Comédie*.

the *Caractères* as self-contained units, independent additions to the moralist's picture of man and society given in the previous section, in spite of La Bruyère's claims that the chapter 'Des Esprits Forts' is the logical conclusion of the whole work. This would at least provide a tidy separation between the two different kinds of 'truth'. But the final chapters are not the only evidence of La Bruyère's refusal to respect the frontier between the realm of reason and that of faith.

What he does at times is to underline the parallelism and the opposition between the two worlds. 'La modestie', for instance, is 'une vertu du dehors', which is an effort to be agreeable to others in hiding one's feelings of superiority over them and should be distinguished from 'l'humilité', 'une vertu surnaturelle', 'un sentiment intérieur qui avilit l'homme à ses propres yeux' ('De l'Homme', 69).

Frequently he moves from one field of reference to the other by an unexpected leap, almost as if he were unaware of the fact. For instance, immediately after having pinpointed, as a moralist, the characteristics of the fool – and very wittily ('Le sot est automate, il est machine, il est ressort...' ('De l'Homme', 42)), La Bruyère, in the following paragraph, introduces a difference between the mind of the fool when alive and in the after-life:

Le sot ne meurt point; ou si cela lui arrive selon notre manière de parler, il est vrai de dire qu'il gagne à mourir, et que dans ce moment où les autres meurent, il commence à vivre. Son âme alors pense, raisonne, infère, conclut, juge, prévoit, fait précisément tout ce qu'elle ne faisait point;...elle va d'égal avec les grandes âmes, avec celles qui font les bonnes têtes ou les hommes d'esprit....(Ibid., 143)

Here we are no longer in the moralist's world. The paradoxical and amusing opening of the paragraph may strike a deceptive note of frivolous witticism. But it is soon clear that we have been carried onto the level of the supernatural where the intellectual possibilities of the mind after death are no longer a question of psychology but a matter of faith.

We may notice how ambiguous the word 'âme' becomes in such a shifting context. Whereas the word was synonymous with mind for the classicists (and the well-known expression 'étude de l'âme humaine' is often used to qualify the psychological investigations of the moralists) La Bruyère uses it in the paragraph above to refer both to the fool's immortal soul and to the mind of men of superior intelligence. This confusion reappears in other places. We may at first have the impression that we see clearly when La Bruyère is giving the word a metaphysical connotation:

Il y a des créatures de Dieu qu'on appelle des hommes, qui ont une âme qui est esprit, dont toute la vie est occupée...à scier du marbre:... (Des Jugements, 102)

but in the next paragraph the distinction between 'soul' and 'mind' becomes blurred:

La plupart des hommes oublient si fort qu'ils ont une âme, et se répandent en tant d'actions et d'exercices où il semble qu'elle est inutile, que l'on croit parler avantageusement de quelqu'un en disant qu'il pense; cet éloge même est devenu vulgaire, qui pourtant ne met cet homme qu'au-dessus du chien ou du cheval. (Ibid., 103)

We suspect that we are back in the world of nature and reason where man, wasting his time in witless occupations, forgets his distinctive natural superiority and neglects to use his brain.

One of the most interesting instances of La Bruyère's sudden moves into a religious context comes in the famous passage on the tulip-fancier ('De la Mode', 2). The man, a slave of fashion, is seen within the framework of human society. After a very concrete description of his behaviour in front of his tulips and a lyrical expression of his ecstasy, at the moment when we are both amused and seduced ourselves by the beauty of the flowers, there comes the stern reminder of higher things:

Dieu et la nature sont en tout cela ce qu'il n'admire point...

and at the end of the passage the religious chord is struck

again, more solemnly, and this time it seems to set off (or to be set off by?) the effect of the *pointe finale*:

Cet homme raisonnable, qui a une âme, qui a un culte et une religion, revient chez soi fatigué, affamé, mais fort content de sa journée: il a vu ses tulipes.

Given these religious preoccupations, which can be perceived more than once throughout the book, it is not surprising that they should have affected La Bruyère's outlook and have had some influence on that side of the *Caractères* which is concerned with *instruire*.

'Instruire': reality and ideal

On ne doit parler, on ne doit écrire que pour l'instruction. (Préface to the *Caractères*)

In a way there is nothing new in this statement. We are familiar with the 'plaire et instruire' of the classicist writers. We know also what they meant by 'instruire'. Not only did they affirm that there was nothing in their works which went against accepted morality but they also implied – and even stated clearly at times – that they had something of value to offer to their readers. But here an important distinction has to be kept in mind. What they presented the reader with was a clearsighted appraisal of the human condition. They did not try to convert, they did not preach. A moralist is not a *moralisateur*.

A substantial part of the *Caractères* is inspired by a similar desire to investigate man's behaviour and his inner nature as they appear to the impartial observer. There are in fact a number of remarks which remind us of La Rochefoucauld. La Bruyère comes back several times to the basic self-centredness of our actions. He stresses the discrepancy between apparent virtues and the real motivation which lies beneath:

Nous faisons par vanité ou par bienséance les mêmes choses, et avec les mêmes dehors, que nous les ferions par inclination ou par devoir... ('De l'Homme', 64)

103

Nor does he fail to note the impotence of will-power where human passions are concerned:

L'on n'est pas plus maître de toujours aimer qu'on l'a été de ne pas aimer. ('Du Cœur', 31)

Was La Bruyère influenced by the *Maximes*?[1] He denies it in his preface, and although it is in the chapter 'Du Cœur' that he seems to come nearest to La Rochefoucauld, we should not overstress the resemblance. The passion of love extends over a great many *terres inconnues* and La Bruyère's own insight into the working of the human heart gives us at times the shock of a new, illuminating discovery.

Such is the case for instance in the following lines which Proust, quite rightly, found admirable:

Les hommes souvent veulent aimer, et ne sauraient y réussir: ils cherchent leur défaite sans pouvoir la rencontrer, et, si j'ose ainsi parler, ils sont contraints de demeurer libres. ('Du Cœur', 16)[2]

The self-defeating pursuit of love and its result is superbly rendered here through the most forceful paradoxes.

La Bruyère however does not limit himself to a lucid study of the inexorable laws which rule man's feelings and man's conduct. He is also concerned with contributing to the moral improvement of his readers. And that not only as a duty which might interfere with his artistic preoccupations but also, on the contrary – questionable as this is – because the moral effect on the reader is for him the supreme test of the literary masterpiece:

Quand une lecture vous élève l'esprit, et qu'elle vous inspire des sentiments nobles et courageux, ne cherchez pas une autre règle pour juger l'ouvrage; il est bon, et fait de main d'ouvrier. ('Des Ouvrages de l'Esprit', 31)

This is a little disturbing on the part of a rather fastidious critic of literature. Yet the very term La Bruyère uses 'fait de

---

[1] For a good clarification of this problem of possible influences or common themes see André Stegman's summary (op. cit., pp. 165–8).

[2] Diffidently Proust suggested a slight alteration to the sentence: 'veulent être aimés' instead of 'veulent aimer'. Not only would this modify the meaning of the maxim but the substitution of a passive form for an active one would certainly weaken considerably the impact of the remark.

main d'ouvrier' (referring to mastery in craftsmanship) to express the perfection of a book compels us to take the statement very seriously; we know the importance he attaches to the technical side of writing ('C'est un métier que de faire un livre, comme de faire une pendule...' (Ibid., 3)).

Moreover, other passages in the same chapter stress the importance of the edifying purpose of literature. La Bruyère suggests that novels and plays 'pourraient être aussi utiles qu'ils sont nuisibles' and that a young girl should look up to examples of constancy, virtue and disinterestedness mirrored in literary works and thus arm herself against the world around her (ibid., 53).

Inevitably La Bruyère's religious outlook moves him to connect the shortcomings of human behaviour with lack of piety and to bracket knowledge of oneself with knowledge of God, as can be seen in this echo of Pascal's 'divertissement':

Tout notre mal vient de ne pouvoir être seuls; de là, le jeu, le luxe, la dissipation, le vin, les femmes, l'ignorance, la médisance, l'envie, l'oubli de soi-même et de Dieu. ('De l'Homme', 99)

Inevitably also he yields to the temptation to cross the line which separates the moralist from the *moralisateur*:

Il n'y a pour l'homme qu'un vrai malheur, qui est de se trouver en faute, et d'avoir quelque chose à se reprocher. (Ibid., 136)

We cannot fail to hear the moralising tone of the lay preacher.

La Bruyère's views on ethics are also different from those of the other moralists in another respect: his relative optimism concerning the moral potentialities of man. Is it because he looks beyond the evidence of the moralist that, although well aware of the many 'fausses vertus', he can believe in the occasional goodness of human nature?

Il y a de certains grands sentiments, de certaines actions nobles et élevées, que nous devons moins à la force de notre esprit qu'à la bonté de notre naturel. ('Du Cœur', 79)

105

A statement which stands in blatant opposition to La Roche-foucauld's assertion that, on the contrary, the 'force de notre esprit' accounts for some greatness and apparent goodness in us.

More than once La Bruyère mentions the existence of natural virtues in the 'âmes bien nées'[1], capable of compassion ('De l'Homme', 80), in the 'grandes âmes' who are above abuse, injustice, suffering and derision (ibid., 81). Although referring in many places to the presence of self-interest, he looks for true merit in the motivation of an action.

Le motif seul fait le mérite des actions des hommes, et le dés-intéressement y met la perfection ('Du Mérite Personnel', 41)

This positive statement seems to imply that there is such a thing as a disinterested action. We find the same positive ring in the following passage, which establishes a kind of hierarchy within the various aspects of human goodness:

Celui-là est bon qui fait du bien aux autres; s'il souffre pour le bien qu'il fait, il est très bon; s'il souffre de ceux à qui il a fait ce bien, il a une si grande bonté qu'elle ne peut être augmentée que dans le cas où ses souffrances viendraient à croître; et s'il en meurt, sa vertu ne saurait aller plus loin: elle est héroïque, elle est parfaite. (Ibid., 44)

Commenting on these lines, Robert Garapon sees in them a reminiscence of the Gospel[2] and one would agree that the kind of altruism depicted here (and the belief in the intrinsic merit attached to suffering) is very near the self-denial, even the self-sacrifice of Christian charity.

An ideal? Probably, but not given as unattainable. The process of idealisation may go further, when La Bruyère presents us with the portraits of perfect human beings. He does so in his lengthy portrait of the perfect ruler ('Du Sou-verain ou De la République', 35), of the perfect woman ('Des Jugements', 28), in his mention of some supermen whose qualities, and particularly their virtue, are dazzlingly resplen-

[1] 'Bien nées' refers here to an innate nobility of mind and not of rank.
[2] See footnote 2, p. 111.

dent. One might argue, of course, that the presentation of the ideal sovereign as an epitome of all virtues and as a defender of the true religion is no more than a conventional set piece destined to flatter Louis XIV. It might equally be said that the idealised portrait of Arthénice is a disguised compliment to a lady known personally to the author. Was La Bruyère thinking of Richelieu, as was remarked by an eighteenth-century scholar, when he wrote:

Il apparaît de temps en temps sur la surface de la terre des hommes rares, exquis, qui brillent par leur vertu, et dont les qualités émi-nentes jettent un éclat prodigieux. Semblables à ces étoiles extra-ordinaires dont on ignore les causes, et dont on sait encore moins ce qu'elles deviennent après avoir disparu, ils n'ont ni aïeuls, ni descendants; ils composent seuls toute leur race. ('Du Mérite Per-sonnel', 22)

I doubt whether the charge of flattery or the suggestion of a *clef* can altogether account for these passages. It is much more probable that La Bruyère is attempting what, as we have seen, he hopes drama or the novel may achieve when they provide examples of virtue, of 'si beaux et si parfaits caractères' ('Des Ouvrages de l'Esprit', 53) for our edification. Once more, in a work devoted to the picture of so many human shortcomings, he feels the need to escape from the closed world of the moralist and to create patterns of perfection, looking up beyond pessimism to those 'étoiles extraordinaires', a beautiful and fitting simile.

EMERGENCE OF THE 'MOI'

The way in which La Bruyère's own beliefs show through his study of man and of contemporary morals points to the importance of the personal element in the *Caractères*. Before examining other aspects of the book it is interesting to note the outward signs which, even at the very surface of the work, reveal the disruptive presence of the author's personality.

I do not mean that the book is autobiographical in the usual

connotation of the term[1] any more than were La Rochefoucauld's *Maximes*, nor that the external data of his life would
confirm or substantiate his remarks. I only mean that in a
number of passages La Bruyère has chosen to give as his own
reactions the views he expresses on man and society.

Of course all moralists use their own knowledge of life and
of themselves. But as a rule they establish a considerable
distance between their own experience and their writing.
Personal experience becomes indistinguishable from the general picture of human nature. Idiosyncrasies of temperament
remain hidden. Even if at times La Fontaine seems to abolish
the distance, we should not be deceived by the tone of
confidential intimacy. These 'fausses confidences' are little
more than stylistic devices.[2]

Admittedly this is often the case also with La Bruyère, the
intrusion of the author into a portrait being a literary device
destined to achieve an effect of immediacy, to show the man
he satirises caught, so to speak, in the act.

For instance, we are given a reported conversation between
the author and Acis, the man who expresses himself in an
incomprehensible and pretentious gibberish:

Que dites-vous? Comment? Je n'y suis pas; vous plairait-il de
recommencer? J'y suis encore moins. Je devine enfin: vous voulez,
Acis, me dire qu'il fait froid; que ne disiez-vous: 'Il fait froid?'. . . ('De
la Société', 7)

Elsewhere it is a dialogue with an anonymous interlocutor
who praises the magnificent attire of a rich dandy:

L'or éclate, dites-vous, sur les habits de *Philémon*. – Il éclate de
même chez les marchands. – Il est habillé des plus belles étoffes. – Le
sont-elles moins toutes déployées dans les boutiques et à la pièce? –
Mais la broderie et les ornements y ajoutent encore la magnificence.
– Je loue donc le travail de l'ouvrier... ('Du Mérite Personnel', 27)

---

[1] André Stegman, commenting on the presence of La Bruyère in the *Caractères*, finds
an excellent phrase when he notes that what transpires from 'confidences indirectes'
is 'non la personne, mais la personnalité de La Bruyère' (op. cit., p. 217).

[2] When he seems to come nearer to personal revelations, in his 'Discours à Madame
de la Sablière', one of his poetic masterpieces, what he does in this assumed self-portrait
is to create, superbly, his own legend.

There follow the details of Philémon's beautiful ornaments; watch, walking-stick, ring, etc. and the last comment of the author:

Vous m'inspirez enfin de la curiosité; il faut voir du moins des choses si précieuses: envoyez-moi cet habit et ces bijoux de Philémon; je vous quitte de la personne.

The writer thus appears as a privileged witness, as a *meneur de jeu*, almost at times as an *agent provocateur*, so close to what he pictures that he is himself part of the picture.

It even happens that the place he occupies among those he portrays is given some kind of concrete localisation:

Démophile, *ò ma droite*, se lamente et s'écrie:...Mais, *ò ma gauche*, Basilide met tout d'un coup sur pied une armée de trois cent mille hommes;...('Du Souverain', 11) (My italics)

In another passage a reference to a chance encounter emphasises the impression of the author running into his characters according to the casual pattern of everyday life:

Théocrine sait des choses assez inutiles;...Le hasard fait que je lui lis mon ouvrage, il l'écoute...('Des Ouvrages de l'Esprit', 25)

The reader himself is made to participate in the scene, sometimes by means of a brief interpolation in the dialogue ('me direz-vous'), at other times in such a way that the nearness of author and reader becomes a physical reality:

...Vous abordez cet homme, ou vous entrez dans cette chambre; je vous tire par votre habit, et vous dis à l'oreille:... ('De la Société', 7)

All the passages I have just mentioned are evidently illustrations of a literary technique the significance of which can be interpreted in different ways, and I shall come back to this later. But the recurrence of this dialogue pattern seems to indicate that the author assumes a part in the play-acting. He may even come very much to the front of the stage when, using his own family tree, he impersonates the man who claims his rights to titles of nobility on the flimsiest evidence:

Je le déclare nettement, afin que l'on s'y prépare et que personne un jour n'en soit surpris: s'il arrive jamais que quelque grand me trouve digne de ses soins; si je fais enfin une belle fortune, il y a un Geoffroy de la Bruyère, que toutes les chroniques rangent au nombre des plus grands seigneurs de France qui suivirent GODEFROY DE BOUILLON à la conquête de la Terre-Sainte: voilà alors de qui je descends en ligne directe. ('De Quelques Usages', 14)

Where he really steals the show is in the lengthy portrait of the philosopher and man of letters, always ready to interrupt his most serious occupations to give a generous welcome to a visitor (in contrast to the man full of his own importance whose door remains shut while he does nothing more than sign a few business papers):

Venez dans la solitude de mon cabinet: la philosophe est accessible; je ne vous remettrai point à un autre jour. Vous me trouverez sur les livres de Platon qui traitent de la spiritualité de l'âme...j'admire Dieu dans ses ouvrages, et je cherche, par la connaissance de la vérité, à régler mon esprit et devenir meilleur. Entrez,...Quelle interruption heureuse pour moi que celle qui vous est utile!... ('Des Biens de Fortune', 12)

The self-portrait is stylised, even idealised, but the persona chosen here reflects some of La Bruyère's own concerns, such as his religious attitude, his passion for reading and the importance he attaches to moral improvement.

This is the point where the distinction between play-acting and self-revelation tends to become blurred. In many places elsewhere in the book there is little ambiguity left. As we go through the *Caractères* we notice how often a judgement, a feeling is given straightforwardly as the author's own. The *moi*, the *je* asserts itself.

As I have already said, the usual method of the moralist is to alter considerably the raw material of his own experience to achieve an impersonal statement stamped with the seal of universality. This implies a strict control of the spontaneous reaction, a rejection of the accidental and the idiosyncratic. La Bruyère breaks through the barriers of such literary conventions, almost giving the impression of reversing the process, of turning a general judgement on man into a single item of personal experience.

Individual moods come to the surface. It may be a movement of exasperation against the condition of men of letters:

Qu'on ne me parle jamais d'encre, de papier, de plume, de style, d'imprimeur, d'imprimerie... Je renonce à tout ce qui a été, qui est, et qui sera livre. *Bérylle* tombe en syncope à la vue d'un chat, et moi à la vue d'un livre... ('Des Jugements', 21)

or an impulse to make a provoking declaration of principle:

Le peuple n'a guère d'esprit, et les grands n'ont point d'âme:... Faut-il opter? Je ne balance pas: je veux être peuple. ('Des Grands', 25)

A fact of his personal experience is noted together with his own reactions to it:

Ce qui me soutient et me rassure contre les petits dédains que j'essuie quelquefois des grands et de mes égaux, c'est que je me dis à moi-même: 'Ces gens n'en veulent peut-être qu'à ma fortune, et ils ont raison: elle est bien petite. Ils m'adoreraient sans doute si j'étais ministre. ('De la Cour', 58)

Perhaps if, as I suggested, we consider the *Caractères* as some kind of diary, we shall understand better the reason for so many remarks where the personal element has the immediacy of what has been freshly experienced. And also a diary is not only made up of the stray impressions or thoughts of the day. It is often a way of working out, on paper, personal problems. Thus the passages in 'Des Esprits Forts' in which La Bruyère endeavours to prove the existence of God may not appear very convincing nor very original. One doubts whether they would convert any *libertin*. But they take on another colour if we think of them as the result of La Bruyère clarifying his own position on the subject. We cannot grudge any man, even if he is not a great and original thinker, the right to work out his metaphysical problems. The 'Je sens qu'il y a un Dieu, et je ne sens pas qu'il n'y en ait point...' ('Des Esprits Forts', 15) is not here a mere echo of Pascal but a *cri du cœur*.

One could easily multiply the examples of statements which take the form of the *je*. There are other signs too of that pressure exerted by the *moi* of the author. Certain mannerisms of style are, I think, rather revealing.

One is the recurrent use of the interrogative sentence, preferably with a cumulative effect:

Qui règle les hommes dans leur manière de vivre et d'user des aliments? la santé et le régime? cela est douteux; une nation entière mange les viandes après les fruits, une autre fait tout le contraire; quelques-uns commencent leurs repas par de certains fruits et les finissent par d'autres, est-ce raison? est-ce usage? Est-ce par un soin de leur santé que les hommes s'habillent jusques au menton...eux qui ont eu si longtemps la poitrine découverte? Est-ce par bienséance?... ('De Quelques Usages', 73)

The paragraph goes on with a series of questions. This pattern, more or less extended in the many different illustrations we can find in the book is not just a device to give an added touch of briskness to the text and to quicken the pace of the passage. The liveliness of the tone tends to modify the relation between author and reader. We have already seen how La Bruyère sometimes drags the reader, literally ('je vous tire par votre habit'), into the little scene of his choice. Now he presses him with questions. Rhetorical questions? Yes and no. The truly rhetorical question is directed nowhere in particular. La Bruyère's interrogations have a more definite target, sometimes one of his characters, often the reader, as if the author, in coming nearer and nearer to him with his repeated demands for an answer, was zealously overdoing his part in the – so far – one-sided dialogue.

The interrogative sentence seems like the outward manifestation of some kind of recurrent rhythm in the author's mind, and translates, at times with a great acceleration of tempo, an impatient desire to query the absurdities of human behaviour, to shake the reader out of his passivity, to initiate the impossible debate between author and reader.

Less noticeable perhaps, but curiously significant of another kind of pressure exerted by the *moi*, is the recurrent semi-apologetic 'j'ose dire' or 'si j'ose dire':

Il y a même des stupides, et j'ose dire des imbéciles... ('Des Biens de Fortune', 38)

Un vieil auteur, et dont j'ose rapporter ici les propres termes... ('De la Cour', 54)

It is as if the author, consciously or half-consciously, aware of his own daring, suggests that his thought, his imagination, has carried him beyond what was generally accepted: resulting in either an unexpected simile or metaphor:

Si j'osais faire une comparaison entre deux conditions tout à fait inégales, je dirais qu'un homme de cœur pense à remplir ses devoirs à peu près comme le couvreur songe à couvrir;... ('Du Mérite Personnel', 16)

Ils n'ont pas, si je l'ose dire, deux pouces de profondeur; si vous les enfoncez, vous rencontrez le tuf. ('De la Cour', 83)

or a bold flight into the future:

...quelles choses nouvelles nous sont inconnues dans les arts, dans les sciences, dans la nature, et j'ose dire dans l'histoire! Quelles découvertes ne fera-t-on point! ('Des Jugements', 107)

Or else a tentative effort to resolve the inconsistencies of our reactions:

On ouvre un livre de dévotion, et il touche; on en ouvre un autre qui est galant, et il fait son impression. Oserai-je dire que le cœur seul concilie les choses contraires, et admet les incompatibles? ('Du Cœur', 73)

So far I have done little more than point out the most superficial manifestations of the author's *moi*. This restless, impulsive *moi* of La Bruyère, ready to respond to all the stimuli of the world around him and within him, considerably modifies the moralist's universe, introduces new dimensions and imposes on it the stamp of a very complex personality.

6

SENSIBILITY

MOODS

The *cœur*, we remember, was for La Rochefoucauld the most mysterious part of the self, perhaps the most precious, the most treacherous also in our quest for truth; and therefore La Rochefoucauld keeps his distance, imposes a check on his sensibility, even in the self-torturing look he casts into the possibilities of this tantalising heart:

S'il est un amour pur et exempt du mélange de nos autres passions, c'est celui qui est caché au fond de notre cœur et que nous ignorons nous-mêmes. (69)

It seems that La Bruyère does not altogether accept such an austere discipline. The relative freedom of expression given to the reactions of his sensibility is a well known feature of his work, so much so that we might be tempted to think that in the *Caractères* we are allowed to witness what, in the writings of the true moralist, was only to be guessed at.

Yet to emphasise a lack of control is too negative a comment. We run the risk of missing the point of what La Bruyère intends to express.

It is perhaps more illuminating to consider another kind of difference between him and La Rochefoucauld. We know how the latter, in his investigation of man's sensibility, constantly proceeds in an inward direction, trying to go deeper and deeper through the various layers of illusion and deception, trying to reach in the invisible recesses of our heart the pure essence of an untainted passion. With La Bruyère the search is directed outwards, no longer towards the core of our sensibility but towards the many facets of its manifestations. The attentive and controlled (for there is control here too) observations are

114

focussed not so much on passions as on emotions and moods.[1]

He is fascinated by those passing moments when our sensibility, roused by some external stimulus, becomes overwhelmingly active and chooses the particular colouring of our thoughts. Here I will mention again the lines I quoted in the preceding chapter:

On ouvre un livre de dévotion et il touche; on en ouvre un autre qui est galant, et il fait son impression. Oserai-je dire que le cœur seul concilie les choses contraires, et admet les incompatibles? ('Du Cœur', 73)

There is a note of puzzlement at the way we react so rapidly and, for a time, so thoroughly, to a prompting from outside, at the rapid succession of contrary moods. What strange alchemy in our heart can absorb into some basic unity such unstable and antagonistic elements?

The word 'touche', although used here figuratively, is significant of that contact through which the physical world affects us. We find it again when La Bruyère remarks on the particular attraction some places have for us, not because they are objectively beautiful – which would of course provoke our admiration – but because of some mysterious affinity between them and our own sensibility:

Il y a des lieux que l'on admire; il y en a d'autres qui touchent, et où on aimerait vivre. ('Du Cœur', 82)

It is in terms of a sensation which turns into an emotion that La Bruyère opposes to the sight of a beautiful face offered for general admiration the sound of a voice which reveals its delicate harmony to our heart alone:

Un beau visage est le plus beau de tous les spectacles; et l'harmonie la plus douce est le son de voix de celle que l'on aime. ('Des Femmes', 10)

What provokes the reactions of our sensibility in the world around us may be something as intangible as the perception of a presence:

---

[1] Even if a part of his work is, as we have seen, an exploration of the passion of love rather similar to that we found in the *Maximes*.

115

Etre avec des gens qu'on aime, cela suffit; rêver, leur parler, ne leur parler point, penser à eux, penser à des choses indifférentes, mais auprès d'eux, tout est égal. ('Du Cœur', 23)

This is the perfect expression of an indefinable feeling of happiness. As a matter of fact happiness is not mentioned. 'Cela suffit', 'tout est égal' are the right words to translate the even tenor of such a mental state. The deliberate use of the plural 'des gens qu'on aime', a refusal to particularise (friends? lovers?), the carefully patterned enumeration which stresses the irrelevance of what we might consider relevant distinctions, everything here is calculated to make room for what is in itself indescribable and to give us its quintessence.

The passages I have commented on show a preference for the nuances of our emotions. They are suffused with a flavour of delicate tenderness. The finer shades of our sensibility, the most subtle joys it can afford us, have for La Bruyère an immense value in our dealings with other people:

L'esprit de la conversation consiste bien moins à en montrer beaucoup qu'à en faire trouver aux autres;...et le plaisir le plus délicat est de faire celui d'autrui. ('De la Société', 16)

Thus pleasure colours a form of self-denial. The satisfaction our sensibility can give us prompts La Bruyère to forget for a time that the motivation of a good deed is of doubtful quality. We are left to enjoy, without *arrière-pensée*, the tender emotion which accompanies an apparently altruistic gesture:

Il y a du plaisir à rencontrer les yeux de celui à qui l'on vient de donner. ('Du Cœur', 45)

Here again it is the physical presence, even the slight particularised detail – eyes meet – which arouses the emotion. We may also note that the moral value of an action is perceived, and perhaps assessed, by sentiment. We saw how La Bruyère's moral outlook was strongly influenced by his Christian beliefs. We see now – and it will appear more forcibly later – that some of his moral reactions are inextricably mixed with the promptings of his heart.

Given the value La Bruyère attaches to the manifestations of our sensibility, and more particularly its spontaneous reactions, we are not surprised to find in the section devoted to literature some mention of what we call the esthetic emotion. Should we not preserve it in all its pristine freshness? Literary criticism, he fears, could become an entrancing intellectual game, exciting for its own sake, and as such prevent us from experiencing an esthetic shock in the presence of a great work of art:

Le plaisir de la critique nous ôte celui d'être vivement touchés de très belles choses. ('Des Ouvrages de l'Esprit', 20)

And if we are moved by a play on the stage why should we be ashamed of our emotion and of tears – those physiological reactions which are an integral part of emotion?

D'où vient que l'on rit si librement au théâtre, et que l'on a honte d'y pleurer?... l'effet naturel du grand tragique serait de pleurer tous franchement... ('Des Ouvrages de l'Esprit, 50)

Thus we owe to our sensibility pleasant moods and precious emotions, including those delectable tears we shed at the theatre. But those are *moments privilégiés*. A great deal of the time as we read the book we come across very different moods: melancholy, frustration, even bitterness. The external world rarely grants the pressing demands of our feelings.

The generous impulses of our heart are sadly checked by circumstances:

Il est triste d'aimer sans une grande fortune, et qui nous donne les moyens de combler ce que l'on aime,... ('Du Cœur', 20)

The feelings of love which we would so much like to indulge are precisely those which are prohibited. Of course virtue should have a more enticing charm for us, but how cold and dull its attraction compared with what we desire, and, what is more, we rightly desire:

Il y a quelquefois dans le cours de la vie de si chers plaisirs et de si tendres engagements que l'on nous défend, qu'il est naturel de

117

désirer du moins qu'ils fussent permis: de si grands charmes ne peuvent être surpassés que par celui de savoir y renoncer par vertu. (Ibid., 85)

No open revolt here, but a subdued protest, a painful sigh, a muffled and lingering regret for some might-have-been.

Perhaps we should not expect any happy encounter, however brief, between what our heart desires and what life has to give. The timing of favourable circumstances works against us. Whereas La Rochefoucauld saw a kind of neutral determinism in our individual destinies, La Bruyère suspects the existence of hostile patterns and remarks ruefully:

Les choses les plus souhaitées n'arrivent point; ou si elles arrivent, ce n'est ni dans le temps ni dans les circonstances où elles auraient fait un extrême plaisir. (Ibid., 62)

Some historians of literature have seen in the *Caractères* the first signs of that awakening of sensibility which is an accepted feature of the eighteenth century. They may be right. There is however no trace of *sentimentality* in the book. The lucid moralist still controls the aspirations of the heart: sensibility sets forth its exacting demands and sadly acknowledges its own limitations:

Il devrait y avoir dans le cœur des sources inépuisables de douleur pour de certaines pertes. Ce n'est guère par vertu ou par force d'esprit que l'on sort d'une grande affliction; l'on pleure amèrement, et l'on est sensiblement touché; mais l'on est ensuite si faible ou si léger que l'on se console. (Ibid., 35)

Unlike La Rochefoucauld, La Bruyère does not question the genuine quality of our grief and our tears, but both of them know that they yearn in vain for an ideal form of sensibility, be it the pure love hidden too deep for us to discover or an inexhaustible springing forth of emotions, which can be called on.

TOWARDS THE LITERATURE OF INDIGNATION

La Bruyère's altruistic impulses deserve some further comments. We have already seen his fondness for the reactions of our sensibility which associate the pleasure bestowed on others with the satisfaction of self. Human sympathy is clearly present in many passages of the *Caractères* – sympathy taken in its original meaning which implies the faculty of feeling for others as one would feel for oneself.

There is in the chapter 'De l'Homme' a group of remarks centred on the problem of compassion. They are the more interesting as La Bruyère approaches the question from different angles and leaves us with the impression that 'to be sorry for other people' is a more complex mental operation than one might suppose.

Genuine compassion for the misfortune of others may require that we ourselves should be at the time in a similar state. As such we can participate as intimately as possible in their suffering – 'entrer dans la misère d'autrui' is the expression used by La Bruyère. On the contrary, people who are rich and in good health lack the personal experience of the evils which afflict others and cannot feel sympathy ('De l'Homme', 79).

They may at least feel uneasy, even ashamed, when face to face with utter wretchedness:

Il y a une espèce de honte d'être heureux à la vue de certaines misères. (Ibid., 82)

'A la vue' is ambiguous. It may mean 'when we see' or it may mean 'when we are seen'. In the first case our shame comes from the unfair contrast we perceive between our happy state and the misery of others. If we choose the second interpretation the implication is slightly different. The feeling of shame springs from the realisation of the effect our visible state of happiness has on those who cannot fail to notice the difference between themselves and us. We look in our own eyes as if we were, albeit unwillingly, flaunting our well-being as an insult. I find it difficult to decide between these two interpretations and am very much tempted to accept them both.

Sympathy is not only a matter of experience and charitable goodwill. It depends at times on the existence in us of certain qualities and among them, perhaps, imagination.

Il semble qu'aux âmes bien nées les fêtes, les spectacles, la symphonie rapprochent et font mieux sentir l'infortune de nos proches ou de nos amis. (Ibid., 80)

This statement may seem surprising. The pleasant atmosphere of a feast, a stage entertainment, or a concert would as a rule divert our thoughts from any sad concern. The seemingly paradoxical nature of the remark comes from the fact that La Bruyère gives us only the final result of a complex mental process without analysing it. That we have here a rather sophisticated and unusual reaction is clear from the reference to the 'âmes bien nées'. It is left to the reader to appreciate the finer sensibility which would respond more intensely to the stimuli of music or beautiful spectacles, the imaginative power which would turn this heightened emotional state into a vicarious experience of our friends' unhappiness while acknowledging the painful contrast between worldly pleasures and private sorrow.

In all these passages the tone is of gentle wistfulness. But human sympathy in the *Caractères* can assume stronger accents:

Il y a des misères qui saisissent le cœur... ('Des Biens de Fortune', 47)

Compare the intensity and the directness of this opening with the more restrained and negative attitude of:

Il y a une espèce de honte d'être heureux à la vue de certaines misères.

Sadness when considering the unfairness of life and the shortcomings of human nature becomes revolt and the compulsive desire to strike back. We can sometimes see the exact point where a generous impulse as well as moral indignation comes to the surface of the text:

L'on doit se taire sur les puissants: il y a presque toujours de la flatterie à en dire du bien; il y a du péril à en dire du mal pendant qu'ils vivent, et de la lâcheté quand ils sont morts. ('Des Grands', 56)

This remark, but for one word, is nothing more than a comment made by a detached observer of court life and is very much a commonplace of worldly wisdom. The word 'lâcheté' breaks the even tenor and neutral tone of the sentence. The observer is no longer detached but lets out the sudden violence of his insulting scorn.

This is just a slight, although significant, indication of the author's ill-contained movements of revulsion. Elsewhere his outspoken revolt against the evils and vices of society and of human nature is at times expressed with such passion and pained bitterness that one can almost see the twitch in the muscles of his face.

Everyone knows the famous passage on the peasants, those 'animaux farouches, des mâles et des femelles, répandus par la campagne, noirs, livides...' ('De l'Homme', 128) but few readers notice the passage which comes immediately before and which is, in my opinion, a much stronger indictment, not only of social injustices in his time, but also of the most horrible feature in man and society – gratuitous cruelty:

Il faut des saisies de terre, et des enlèvements de meubles, des prisons et des supplices, je l'avoue; mais justice, lois et besoin à part, ce m'est une chose toujours nouvelle de contempler avec quelle férocité les hommes traitent d'autres hommes. (Ibid., 127)

This reference to intense personal feeling reveals also to what extent sensibility will reinforce moral judgement in his most violent attacks against evil. In this respect La Bruyère belongs, like Pope or Swift, to what I would call the literature of indignation.

Indignation may take the form of irony, as when he comments on the monstrous inequality of fortune among men, and the even more monstrous indifference of the rich and particularly of the well-fed.

Champagne, au sortir d'un long dîner qui lui enfle l'estomac, et dans les douces fumées d'un vin d'Avenay ou de Sillery, signe un ordre qu'on lui présente, qui ôterait le pain à toute une province si l'on n'y remédiait. Il est excusable: quel moyen de comprendre, dans la première heure de la digestion, qu'on puisse quelque part mourir de faim? ('Des Biens de Fortune', 18)

Note in the brief sketch of Champagne the repulsive gross-ness associated with refined luxury (expanded paunch and expensive wines) in contrast with the plain word bread, a basic, and as such sacred, right of any human being. The final sarcasm is the more cutting as the ironical question which seems to be directed specifically at Champagne is also bound to strike at all of us.

The attack against the wealthy, and particularly against some men in whom greed for money supersedes anything else, can be more direct:

Il y a des âmes sales, pétries de boue et d'ordure, éprises du gain et de l'intérêt... ('Des Biens de Fortune', 58)

The invective is singularly violent, with an effect of physical revulsion. Although each of the words 'sales', 'boue', 'ordure' is a conventional metaphor to express moral degradation (more especially the last two), because they are used all three in rapid succession, they recover here part of the concrete effect of dirt, mud and filth.

The use of metaphor to translate scorn is even more forceful and much bolder in some other passages.

In one of the paragraphs of the section 'De la Cour' La Bruyère shows us the courtiers going up and down the stair-case in the residence of an important minister, talking to the latter without having anything to say, moving aside and again whispering something in the minister's ear; and suddenly, in face of this futile activity and the imbecile self-satisfaction on the countenance of the men, La Bruyère's anger bursts out:

Pressez-les, tordez-les, ils dégouttent l'orgueil, l'arrogance, la pré-somption...(61)

Here the metaphor is so powerful that it is almost more than a metaphor. It is the beginning of a gesture, the exasperated gesture of a man wringing those puppets in his hands, crushing them, leaving nothing of them but the thick dripping of a hateful substance.

The scope of the indictment may be enlarged so as to prosecute all men, past and present:

Petits hommes, hauts de six pieds, tout au plus de sept...espèce d'animaux glorieux et superbes, qui méprisez toute autre espèce, qui ne faites même pas comparaison avec l'éléphant et la baleine... ('Des Jugements', 119)

This scornful apostrophe is the beginning of a long fragment in which La Bruyère upbraids the presumption of the human race, points out derisively its frivolity and insignificance, denounces the stupidity and cruelty of warns, and as a final thrust sneers at men's unwise and abject submission to the voice of power if it is loud enough. It is a carefully constructed passage, with a skilful blend of oratorical tone in the manner of the 'grand style' and of the more broken rhythm of the conversational style. The author's emotion is perhaps less perceptible than in some of the illustrations I have already mentioned. La Bruyère has obviously enjoyed renewing the traditional topic of animals' superiority over man by means of picturesque touches. One might add that in the last part of the fragment he has narrowed the field of his relentless attack by choosing William of Orange as the prototype of the spurious conqueror. But the impact of passionate urgency can still be felt in more than one sentence. The black humour of the assumed matter of fact description of the effect of bombardment:

...de petits globes...qui vous coupent en deux parts ou qui éventrent, sans compter ceux qui tombant sur vos toits, enfoncent les planchers, vont du grenier à la cave, en enlèvent les voûtes, et font sauter en l'air, avec vos maisons, vos femmes qui sont en couche, l'enfant et la nourrice...

has that deliberate touch of cruelty which is so often the most revealing sign of strongly felt indignation.

What makes this indignation more bitter at times is the confession of helplessness. The moralist ought to be more patient with human nature, given the incontrovertible fact that he cannot change it: 'Ne nous emportons point contre les hommes en voyant leur dureté, leur ingratitude, leur injustice...' says La Bruyère at the beginning of the section 'De l'Homme' – this, of course, in contradiction with his frequent outbursts – 'Ils sont ainsi faits, c'est leur nature.' The fact is acknowledged. But for all that, sensibility is not checkmated. Bitterness remains and can still denounce with sarcasm the irrelevance of virtue in the high spheres of power: '...que voulez-vous quelquefois que l'on fasse d'un homme de bien?' ('De la Cour', 53).

There is perhaps a last resort when the sight of an iniquitous society and the evidence of ferocious selfishness become unbearably painful:

Il y a des misères sur la terre qui saisissent le cœur; il manque à quelques-uns jusqu'aux aliments; ils redoutent l'hiver, ils appréhendent de vivre...de simples bourgeois, seulement à cause qu'ils étaient riches, ont eu l'audace d'avaler en un seul morceau la nourriture de cent familles. ('Des Biens de Fortune', 47)

and La Bruyère adds:

Tienne qui voudra contre de si grandes extrémités; je ne veux être, si je le puis, ni malheureux ni heureux; je me jette et me réfugie dans la médiocrité.

This is a reluctant admission of defeat and the ultimate move: the desperate impulse to escape any responsibility for the cruel working of society and to place himself neither among the torturers nor among their victims.

I do not suppose that La Bruyère had any practical suggestions to put forward in order to reform society. It is tempting to see in him a forerunner of the political thinkers of the eighteenth century. The evidence of all the passages concerned with political institutions and practice points to a conservative ideal of a good Christian monarch. But he certainly expressed a burning desire that men and society might be other than they were. The positive improvement he aimed at achieving concerns not the mechanism of society but the individual conscience.

This passionate wish to convince men of their moral short-comings and this strong vein of indignation explain why, when La Bruyère's vision of the world is a comic one – as is often the case – this comic vision is, a great deal of the time, very different from the kind of comedy to be found in Molière or La Fontaine. The pure comic vision achieved by those writers, is a gratuitous intellectual pleasure which presupposes an attitude of complete detachment assumed by the author and enjoyed by the reader or spectator. It may lead to some upsetting afterthoughts but for the time being, while we enjoy it, sensibility is, so to speak, anaesthetized.

Most of the time La Bruyère is not in a mood of detachment, nor is his purpose to create such a mood in the reader. Quite the reverse: comic devices such as irony or humour are destined to provoke indignation, scorn or loathing, which is the same as saying that La Bruyère is a satirist.[1] The satirist does not use comedy in a disinterested way; he has a moral purpose, which is to correct men by showing them their vices and follies as ridiculous.

We have already seen La Bruyère's moral preoccupations and his tendency to be at times a *moralisateur* rather than a moralist. The didactic intention he expresses in several passages, particularly in the 'Discours sur Théophraste', is more than part of the traditional 'plaire et instruire'. His method of instruction as stated in the *Discours* is very much in keeping with the satiric mode. What he has to offer is the kind of work, centred on the 'mœurs du temps', in which authors 'corrigent les hommes les uns par les autres, par ces images de choses

---

[1] There are elements of satire in Molière and La Fontaine, but they are usually incidental to their comic vision. In the case of Molière the only time when one may suspect a direct and central satirical intention is in his personal attack against medicine placed in the mouth of the *raisonneur* in *Le Malade Imaginaire*, and perhaps in Dom Juan's long speech in praise of religious hypocrisy.

qui leur sont si familières, et dont néanmoins ils ne s'avisaient pas de tirer leur instruction'.

Satire is very much concerned with making an immediate impact, hence the preference for topics which are part of the reader's everyday experience. To hit the basic vices and follies of mankind by concentrating the attack on their contemporary manifestations is an efficient tactic as well as a short cut. And, if the satirist hopes to offer some change for the better, it is obviously only the manners and morals of the present day which are relevant to his readers. La Bruyère may give his characters pseudo-classical names, and now and then introduce some local colour borrowed from the times of Greece and Rome; this is a mere literary convention or, better, a passing touch of artistic *coquetterie*. The *Caractères* are essentially what the sub-title indicates: 'Les Mœurs de ce Siècle'.

La Bruyère's portraits are the best known feature of the book, and we may notice what an asset the art of the portrait is to the satirist. As Pope puts it:

To attack Vices in the abstract, without touching persons, may be safe fighting indeed, but it is fighting with Shadows. General propositions are obscure, misty and uncertain, compar'd with plain, full and home examples: Precepts only apply to our Reason, which in most men is but weak: Examples are pictures, and strike the Senses, nay raise the Passions, and call in those (the strongest and most general of all motives) to the aid of reformation. Every vicious man makes the case his own; and that is the only way by which such men can be affected...[1]

There remains the delicate question of the resemblance to truth evinced by the portrait. Commenting on the passage by Pope I have just quoted Reuben A. Brower remarks quite rightly that 'examples may mean "particular cases" or "representative cases"'.[2] The satirist may choose to attack a living man under a fictitious name (or under his real name or initials) or he may be portraying an entirely fictitious character.

[1] *The Correspondence of Alexander Pope*, ed. George Sherburn, 5 vols., Oxford, 1956, (Vol. III, p. 423).
[2] *Alexander Pope, the Poetry of Allusion*, Clarendon Press, 1959, p. 301.

Very occasionally La Bruyère mentions a name or makes it abundantly clear that he has a real man in view. Such is the case when William of Orange (not named but unambiguously recognisable) becomes a particularised illustration of a certain type of sovereign. But in fact the difference between the fictitious and the non-fictitious portrait is as a rule not so clear-cut. Even if the writer at the start had thought of a living individual, the process of stylisation rubs out the realistic features which would otherwise give away the true identity of the portrait and removes the sting of personal offence; unless of course the author intends to be personally offensive, as is the case with some satirists, but rarely with La Bruyère, I think. Stylisation is so evident in most of his portraits that we can ignore the problem of *clefs*. In two additions to his *Préface* he warns the reader not only against 'toute plainte...toute fausse application...' but also against any narrow interpretation of his book. Although he had often taken his characters from the court and from his country:

...on ne peut pas néanmoins les restreindre à une seule cour, ni les renfermer en un seul pays, sans que mon livre ne perde beaucoup de son étendue et de son utilité, ne s'écarte du plan que je me suis fait d'y peindre les hommes en général...[1]

This goes beyond the question of identifying his portraits and raises a different issue. Because of the satirist's concern with immediate reality he runs the risk of doing no more than scratching the surface of the society he ridicules without getting at the fundamental vices. The more topical satire is, the more short-lived. It rapidly loses its relevance, and therefore its impact, and retains only a historical interest. There is in the *Caractères* a certain amount of this kind of satire, inevitably, as La Bruyère is depicting 'les mœurs de ce siècle'. But his stylisation is at times so successful that it enables us to transpose a seventeenth-century folly and see it in terms of our twentieth-century experience (for 'directeur de conscience' read psychiatrist).

[1] Garapon, p. 62.

127

However the importance of satire in the *Caractères* should be judged by its deeper characteristics, and mostly in connexion with the importance of sensibility in the work. Undoubtedly the careful balance that previous moralists had secured between the detachment of the observer and the reactions of sensibility is destroyed. Sensibility takes the upper hand, and with it a sense of urgency develops, an impulse to do something about the state of the world, to protest, to attack, to pillory. In several passages of the *Caractères* La Bruyère has given French literature something which – save for one masterpiece, *Candide* – is singularly lacking in that literature, great satire. Great satire is cruel, and its cruelty is in proportion to the intensity of the indignation felt by the satirist, as if the writer wanted to impose his own suffering on the reader. I would not say that La Bruyère achieves the greatness of Pope or Swift, but we find at times in his book the same kind of satirical vigour, of cruel wording which seems to tear at the heart of man.

7

THEMES AND PATTERNS

There is another feature of the moralist's universe which is considerably altered in the *Caractères*: its historic timelessness. Not that the French classicists were unaware of history, but they had chosen to stop the clock, so to speak, and to consider the civilisation of their times in a kind of historical vacuum, so that the contemporary aspects of their society merged into a more permanent and universal picture. In La Fontaine's *Fables*, for instance, the theme of the tyrant did not refer specifically to Louis XIV. The attitude of the writer implied that there had always been tyrants and that there always would be.

La Bruyère, on the contrary, seems very much preoccupied with the fact that the civilisation of his age is only a dot on the endless line of time, and he feels the double pressure of past and future.

The past weighs heavily on him with the impression that humanity is too old, that it has exhausted all its intellectual possibilities:

Tout est dit, et l'on vient trop tard depuis plus de sept mille ans qu'il y a des hommes, et qui pensent. ('Des Ouvrages de l'Esprit', 1)

How useless, even pernicious, the progress in science and learning since classical antiquity:

Que de choses depuis Varron, que Varron a ignorées! Ne vous suffirait-il pas même de n'être savant que comme Platon ou comme Socrate? ('Des Jugements', 11)

But the pendulum may swing in the opposite direction: far from being too old, humanity is too young, too immature. And whereas none of the previous moralists had dreamed about the future, La Bruyère experiences moments of intense curiosity, mixed with a nuance of frustration and envy, towards the future knowledge of mankind:

Si le monde dure seulement cent millions d'années, il est encore dans toute sa fraîcheur, et ne fait que commencer;...quelles découvertes ne fera-t-on point! quelles différentes révolutions ne doivent pas arriver sur toute la face de la terre, dans les Etats et dans les empires! quelle ignorance est la nôtre! et quelle légère expérience que celle de six ou sept mille ans! (Ibid., 107)

Time, as we have seen, interested La Rochefoucauld in so far as it was part of the conditioning of man's mental make-up: man was seen as a prisoner of time, bound to follow an inescapable pattern.

For La Bruyère time is a source of more haunting questions. It is in itself a subject for speculation, to be viewed from different angles, objectively and subjectively, and it is perhaps the most important dimension in his picture of man and society.

Considerations on time can hardly avoid the great commonplaces. But when remarking on the inevitable process of gradual deterioration in all things La Bruyère gives a twist to the familiar statement and suggests an unfair paradox in the inevitable decay of our mind, destroyed by what sustains it:

L'esprit s'use comme toutes choses: les sciences sont ses aliments, elles le nourrissent et le consument. ('De l'Homme', 92)

Still more unfair for him is the lack of synchronisation between events and our dearest wishes ('Du Cœur', 62). There seems to be some ill-will at work in the timing of favourable occurrences.

Yet the fault may be in our own make-up as well. The future we dream of is always brighter than the present, hence that feeling of anticlimax we experience when we obtain what we have desired with passion:

Il y a de certains biens que l'on désire avec emportement, et dont l'idée seule nous enlève et nous transporte; s'il nous arrive de les obtenir, on les sent plus tranquillement qu'on ne l'eût pensé, on en jouit moins que l'on aspire encore à de plus grands. ('De l'Homme', 29)

There is perhaps an echo of Montaigne in this statement that men are always looking ahead, pursuing a wild-goose-chase after an ever-receding quarry, and are thus unable to enjoy the present. Only children, La Bruyère says, can do so, because they are unaware of time:

Les enfants n'ont ni passé ni avenir, et, ce qui ne nous arrive guère, ils jouissent du présent. ('De l'Homme', 51)

The theme of time is inevitably linked with the topics of old age and death. When dealing with these La Bruyère seems to be particularly struck by men's incapacity to grasp the reality of time and the logical sequence of the 'seven ages' – reduced to three in the *Caractères*[1] – between birth and death. When they look back on their past, the picture they have of their own life is as confused as what one can remember after sleep; the longer the life, the longer the sleep, the more muddled and inconsequent the picture:

... ils confondent leurs différents âges, ils n'y voient rien qui marque assez pour mesurer le temps qu'ils ont vécu. Ils ont eu un songe confus, informe, et sans aucune suite; ils sentent néanmoins, comme ceux qui s'éveillent, qu'ils ont dormi longtemps. (Ibid., 47)

When men look forward to their future the picture is as blurred, and in a way it is a blessing that men cannot take in the relentless movement of time. The inevitability of their own death is partly obliterated by the uncertainty of its precise date; and this uncertainty grows confused in their minds with a vague reassuring impression of timelessness: a perceptive analysis which La Bruyère words admirably in a very fine sentence translating our tenacious if absurd conviction that we shall live for ever:

Ce qu'il y a de certain dans la mort est un peu adouci par ce qui est incertain; c'est un indéfini dans le temps qui tient quelque chose de l'infini et de ce qu'on appelle éternité. (Ibid., 38)

Here speaks the moralist, the student of human nature. But the temporal element assumes an even greater importance in

[1] See in 'De l'Homme' paragraphs 48 and 49.

the book when La Bruyère is concerned not with the basic and permanent features of man but with the most superficial aspects of time: with topical subjects, with those fleeting moments which compose the civilisation of his age – a precarious avatar in the endless succession of constant metamorphoses. It is of course in keeping with his role as a satirist that he should direct his attention to what belongs more specifically to 'les mœurs de ce siècle': political institutions, rivalry between court and town, literary circles, preachers and 'directeurs de conscience', tax-collectors and noblemen. The satirical intention, however, does not altogether account for the particular relief given to contemporary life.

The importance attached to fashion, to the extent of devoting a whole section of the book to it, is significant; the more so when we consider the passage which ends the chapter and which gives a powerful enlargement to the concept of 'mode'. It takes the form of a meditation on time in which the commonplace, superbly expressed, is given an original slant:

Chaque heure en soi comme à notre égard est unique; est-elle écoulée une fois, elle a péri entièrement, les millions de siècles ne la ramèneront pas. Les jours, les mois, les années s'enfoncent et se perdent sans retour dans l'abîme des temps; le temps même sera détruit: ce n'est qu'un point dans les espaces immenses de l'éternité, et il sera effacé. Il y a de légères et frivoles circonstances du temps qui ne sont point stables, qui passent, et que j'appelle des modes, la grandeur, la faveur, les richesses, la puissance, l'autorité, l'indépendance, le plaisir, les joies, la superfluité. Que deviendront ces modes quand le temps même aura disparu? La vertu seule, si peu à la mode, va au delà du temps. ('De la Mode', 31)

The passage is built on forceful contrasts; the importance of one hour is measured against millions of centuries, months and years against eternity, the fragile avatars of human concerns against the solidity of virtue. In spite of the pious conclusion, it is clear that La Bruyère is overwhelmingly interested in these 'légères et frivoles circonstances du temps', these superfluities. The opening sentence leaves no doubt: 'chaque heure...est unique', *per se* ('en soi') and for us. Its very vulnerability opposes the all-powerful forces which will destroy it. The positive value of its uniqueness – the infinite price of the irreplaceable – stands out against the negating process which erases all distinctive marks, all categories of time, and time itself. As for the frivolous 'modes' enumerated in a descending order of magnitude, it seems that their attractiveness increases as their objective importance decreases, as if their very lightness were a challenge to the ponderous threat of annihilation.

There are other passages in the book where we see La Bruyère fascinated by what possesses the characteristic of uniqueness, of singularity; some ridiculous traits in men, for instance:

...qui par leur singularité ne tirent point à conséquence, et ne sont d'aucune ressource pour l'instruction et pour la morale!...vices uniques...qui sont moins de l'humanité que de la personne. ('De l'Homme', 158)

This is the point where satire loses its basic purpose, where there appears to be a change of focus in La Bruyère's study of man. I shall come back to it – to this shift from the universal to the particular. Here I am dealing with a parallel move: the shift from the permanent to the ephemeral.

More than once La Bruyère expresses concern about the effects of time on things he values. Some aspects of civilisation seem to him particularly threatened by time. Are books safe? If a literary work is good should it not survive? We know of course that in the famous 'Querelle des Anciens et des Modernes' La Bruyère was on the side of the classics. But there is all the same a trace of concern when he reflects on the fact that 'nous qui sommes si modernes, serons anciens dans quelques siècles' ('Discours sur Théophraste'), and elsewhere he wonders about the future fate of the literary masterpieces of his age:

Supposons que notre langue pût un jour avoir le sort de la grecque et de la latine, serait-on pédant, quelques siècles après qu'on ne la parlerait plus, pour lire Molière ou La Fontaine? ('Des Jugements', 19)

A question to be answered in the negative, for it comes after La Bruyère has stated that the only point relevant to survival is the quality of a language or of a work of literature. Nevertheless the question has been asked, and probably with a light shudder of uneasiness.

It is easier to perceive the nuance of tender anxiety in the long passage where he considers the words which are becoming obsolete, those which are already half-dead, those which are about to disappear from current usage:

Certes est beau dans sa vieillesse...*Cil* a été dans ses beaux jours le plus joli mot de la langue française...L'usage a préféré...*pensées* à *pensers*, un si beau mot, et dont le vers se trouvait si bien... ('De Quelques Usages', 73)

Language is vulnerable and there is in La Bruyère the suspicion that beauty and fragility go together, that the spoken word, so ephemeral (*verba volent*) is often more subtle, more satisfactory than the written word:

Il me semble que l'on dit les choses encore plus finement qu'on ne peut les écrire. ('De la Société', 78)

But there is more. In the civilisation of his age there are many things of which he violently disapproves. We have seen how cruel his satire can be. And yet paradoxically it seems that he wants to preserve the precious short-lived quality of the very things he condemns.

This is no easy task. Ways of thinking, of behaving, are so fleeting that they change not only from century to century, from year to year, but also from day to day. The atmosphere of the court, for instance:

Qui peut nommer de certaines couleurs changeantes, et qui sont diverses selon les divers jours dont on les regarde? de même, qui peut définir la cour? ('De la Cour', 3)

It is almost impossible to seize on the particular moment when a man changes from being a *dévôt* to being a *libertin*:

Les couleurs sont préparées, et la toile est toute prête; mais comment le fixer, cet homme inquiet, léger, inconstant, qui change de mille et mille figures? Je le peins dévôt, et je crois l'avoir attrapé; mais il m'échappe, et déjà il est libertin... ('De la Mode', 19)

Was this tantalising elusiveness one more incentive? Whatever the difficulties, La Bruyère attempted to catch the ephemeral quality of one moment in the history of man.

'LE MONDE EXTERIEUR'

The essence of that particular moment is that it is a concrete reality, with its individual colouring. A given civilisation is a world of things – clothes, houses, implements, places – a world of current events and of people in the public eye. French civilisation in the second half of the twentieth century certainly includes things such as typewriters, tape-recorders and electric gadgets, rushing to the Alps for skiing and to the seaside for sun-bathing, a taste for ancient furniture, unisex clothes for the young and an interest in the Tour de France.

We should not of course expect to find in the *Caractères* a straightforward documentary survey of everyday life in France at the end of the seventeenth century. But let us look first at the way in which La Bruyère gives us something of the particular reality of his age indirectly while making fun of a personage who is nothing more than a passionate witness of every topical event, a mirror of a hundred little details of momentary and – for him and many others – momentous importance: fashionable places of entertainment, public executions or celebrations, fairs, religious services, names of currently popular singers, even titles of women's magazines:

Voilà un homme, dites-vous, que j'ai vu quelque part;...je vais, s'il se peut, aider votre mémoire. Est-ce au boulevard sur un strapontin, ou aux Tuileries dans la grande allée, ou dans le balcon à la comédie? Est-ce au sermon, au bal, à Rambouillet? Où pourriez-vous ne l'avoir point vu? où n'est-il point? S'il y a dans la place une fameuse exécution, ou un feu de joie, il paraît à une fenêtre de l'Hôtel de Ville;...s'il se fait un carrousel, le voilà entré, et placé sur l'amphithéâtre; si le Roi reçoit des ambassadeurs, il voit leur marche,... ('De la Ville', 13)

What a loss if such a man happened to die:

Qui annoncera un concert, un beau salut, un prestige de la Foire? Qui vous avertira que Beaumavielle mourut hier; que Rochois est enrhumée, et ne chantera de huit jours?...Qui prêtera aux femmes les *Annales galantes* et le *Journal amoureux*?... (Ibid.)

The passage should be read in its entirety to appreciate to the full the skill of the overall composition and wealth of material included. But even from these extracts we can see some of the devices used by La Bruyère and the effect they are meant to produce: the abrupt beginning which places the reader from the start right in the middle of the turbulent scene to be staged, the accumulation of precise information, the staccato rhythm – a succession of brisk moves to skim the surface of *actualité* – the telescoping of events which accelerates the uncanny rapidity with which the man goes from place to place. What we are given here, quite apart from the satire on a certain form of frivolity, is undoubtedly a remarkable rendering of the ephemeral and exciting quality of immediate reality.

This is just a sample of the stylistic devices used by La Bruyère to achieve the kind of effect I have mentioned. It is evident that such an original and striking presentation of an original picture of human behaviour could only be the work of a conscious artist who had carefully considered the possibilities and impossibilities afforded by the tools of his trade.

Problems of craftsmanship

In a modest way La Bruyère shares with a number of the great figures of literature the distinction of being at the same time a writer and a critic. The chapter 'Des Ouvrages de l'Esprit' and remarks to be found elsewhere in the book are a clear proof of his interest in the technique of writing. The views he expresses are perhaps not sufficient to illuminate a creative process which must have been a particularly complex and delicate operation; nevertheless they constitute helpful pointers.

In many respects La Bruyère belongs to French classicism. Yet even when some of his literary tenets seem to coincide with those of his friend Boileau, the wording of a common principle suggests some interesting dissimilarity.

For instance, La Bruyère's insistence on the professional standard to be expected from a man of letters was certainly shared by all the classicists. It went with the idea of hard work and exacting attention to all the details of the task. But if we compare Boileau's lines:

Cent fois sur le métier remettez votre ouvrage,
Polissez-le sans cesse et le repolissez. (*Art Poétique*)

with La Bruyère's:

C'est un métier de faire un livre, comme de faire une pendule. ('Des Ouvrages de l'Esprit', 3)

we are struck by the difference in tone and expression. Boileau's lines have a kind of neutral elegance. 'Métier' is used figuratively. The meaning is clear but the original tenor of the image – that of a frame for weaving or embroidering – has more or less vanished. This is as well, since it would not fit in with the second image – the polishing or filing of some hard substance – which has a subtle traditional flavour and is meant gently to send the reader back to Horace's *limae labor et mora*. La Bruyère's statement is matter-of-fact and the comparison 'comme de faire une pendule' is intended to give a shock. The word *pendule* is not wrapped up in even the lightest and most transparent film of literary tradition. It stands up uncompromisingly in the unadorned solidity of its everyday existence.

The difference is not just that which separates prose from poetry. It is significant of a wish, on the part of La Bruyère, to experiment in the fields of metaphor and of diction.

We must at this stage remember the limitations set on the classicists' style, and particularly on diction, as I mentioned previously:[1] the restricted vocabulary which only the genius of Racine could make both forceful and poetic through a complex dramatic network of cross-references, the outworn

---

[1] See Chapter 1, pp. 8–9.

literary allusiveness which stood in the way of La Fontaine,[1] the protean flexibility of an abstract terminology which accounted for regrettable ambiguities in some of La Rochefoucauld's analyses.

The classicists did not revolt against such limitations. We saw, however, that La Rochefoucauld was well aware of the shortcomings of the written word when it came to a full and accurate rendering of a given experience. The feeling that some new medium, some new style, was needed prompted La Fontaine to exclaim: 'Il me faut du nouveau, n'en fût-il plus au monde' (*Clymène*). We find the same reaction in La Bruyère at the very beginning of his book:

Tout est dit, et l'on vient trop tard depuis plus de sept mille ans qu'il y a des hommes et qui pensent.

This statement of the writer's complete impotence, of the impossibility of innovation is of course contradicted by all that follows and has the same paradoxical characteristic as La Fontaine's 'n'en fût-il plus au monde'. In both cases it is an assessment, couched in the strongest possible terms, of the almost intolerable burden of an admirable tradition. Indeed 'tout n'est pas dit' and 'tout n'est pas pensé', not only because thought and language are constantly changing but because for the writer the connexion between *dire* and *penser* is precisely where the crucible of literary creation is to be found and where the complex alchemy of multiple elements alters considerably both ways of thinking and forms of expression.

French classicism may appear as a moment of exceptional stability in the evolution of literary language. It is perhaps with La Bruyère that we become conscious of an inevitable tendency to move away from certain accepted linguistic conventions, although it is rather difficult to decide whether it reflected a general drift or was the result of La Bruyère's own approach to problems of literary creation.

We cannot, however, expect from him, any more than from

---

[1] On this point I refer the reader to my studies on La Fontaine (*O Muse fuyante proie*, Paris, Corti, 1962, pp. 153–69) and on Racine (*Racine, or the triumph of relevance*, Cambridge University Press, 1967, pp. 150–60).

any of the previous classicists, a frontal attack against the literary conventions of his age. On the contrary, he expresses the greatest respect and admiration for the language forged by his century and in fact seems to find in its very perfection an incentive (or an excuse?) for experimentation:

L'on écrit régulièrement depuis vingt années; l'on est esclave de la construction; l'on a enrichi la langue de nouveaux mots, secoué le joug du latinisme, et réduit le style à la phrase purement française; l'on a presque retrouvé le nombre que MALHERBE et BALZAC avaient les premiers rencontré, et que tant d'auteurs depuis eux ont laissé perdre; l'on a mis enfin dans le discours tout l'ordre et toute la netteté dont il est capable: cela conduit insensiblement à y mettre de l'esprit. ('Des Ouvrages de l'Esprit', 60)

Sainte-Beuve saw in this paragraph a good summary of the evolution of French prose in the seventeenth century.[1] More interesting are some of the puzzling implications which the wording seems to convey. Regularity, order, clarity are certainly given as praiseworthy qualities. Yet do we not suspect some mental reservation, a curious ambivalence in the references to slavery and liberation? For if, on the one hand, the seventeenth-century writer has 'secoué le joug du latinisme' on the other he is 'esclave de la construction' and has 'réduit le style'. Does this reveal some hesitancy between the blessings of strict rules and those of freedom?

It is most probable that the whole paragraph is carefully worded so as to give particular relief to the last sentence 'cela conduit insensiblement à y mettre de l'esprit', a sentence which is bound to raise difficulties of interpretation. Julien Benda wonders whether La Bruyère is not putting forward here the rather modern theory that thoughts are conditioned by form.[2] I prefer to agree with Robert Garapon who sees *esprit* in this context as a sort of *ingéniosité* which La Bruyère, seeking an excuse for indulging it, presents as the natural outcome of order and clarity.[3] Might we even suppose that, in the opinion

---

[1] *Portraits littéraires*, I, Didier, Paris, 1852, p. 401.
[2] See footnote to his edition of La Bruyère's works (op. cit., p. 680).
[3] See footnote 4, p. 92.

of La Bruyère, the time has come to go beyond a certain form of orderly pattern and that the writer is necessarily led by degrees to evolve a new kind of creative wit?

That such sophistication may happen to bypass the rule of clarity to a certain extent is mentioned in a previous passage:

> Que sert aux lecteurs de comprendre aisément et sans peine des choses frivoles et puériles, quelquefois fades et communes, et d'être moins incertains de la pensée d'un auteur qu'ennuyés de son ouvrage?
> Si l'on jette quelque profondeur dans certains écrits, si l'on affecte une finesse de tour, et quelquefois une trop grande délicatesse, ce n'est que par la bonne opinion qu'on a de ses lecteurs. (Ibid., 57)

The risk is therefore worth taking. Moreover La Bruyère does not stop at the contemporary intelligent reader. Unlike the other classicists, whose respect for the 'goût du siècle' was axiomatic, he adopts a bolder and strangely more modern idea that even if our own age does not do justice to our works:

> ...cette justice qui nous est quelquefois refusée par nos contemporains, la postérité sait nous la rendre. (Ibid., 67)

What encourages a certain boldness in experimenting with style is the important distinction La Bruyère draws between those who write 'par humeur' and the others. He is obviously among the first, among those

> ...que le cœur fait parler, à qui il inspire les termes et les figures, et qui tirent, pour ainsi dire, de leurs entrailles tout ce qu'ils expriment sur le papier... (Ibid., 64)

This is not yet the romantic exclamation 'Ah! frappe-toi le cœur, c'est là qu'est le génie', but is undoubtedly a claim to a subjective approach to the art of writing and a way of opposing such creative activity to a safer imitation of acknowledged masterpieces within accepted canons. Here we find again the emergence of the author's *moi*, leading to the conception of original talent as a jealously guarded preserve of individual characteristics. Such writers as himself do not copy and, conversely, cannot be copied:

... je rirais d'un homme qui voudrait sérieusement parler mon ton de voix, ou me ressembler de visage. (Ibid.)

There is no question, of course, of a straightforward outpouring of the writer's feelings. The criterion of spontaneity is as alien to La Bruyère as to the other classicists, and his conception of naturalness is not different from theirs:

Combien d'art pour rentrer dans la nature! combien de temps, de règles, d'attention et de travail pour danser avec la même liberté et la même grâce que l'on sait marcher; pour chanter comme on parle, parler et s'exprimer comme l'on pense... ('Des Jugements', 34)

To make the expression fit the natural pattern of the thought is the suggested ideal. But how much more difficult it is for the writers who write 'par humeur', since the flashes of inspiration depend on moods, on the transient reactions of the *moi*:

Ceux qui écrivent par humeur sont sujets à retoucher leurs ouvrages: comme elle n'est pas toujours fixe, et qu'elle varie en eux selon les occasions, ils se refroidissent bientôt pour les expressions et les termes qu'ils ont le plus aimés. ('Des Ouvrages de l'Esprit', 17)

As thought varies, so will the manner of expressing it and therefore La Bruyère is led to reject uniformity of style:

On pense les choses d'une manière différente, et on les explique par un tour aussi tout différent, par une sentence, par un raisonnement, par une métaphore ou quelque autre figure, par un parallèle, par une simple comparaison, par un fait tout entier, par un seul trait, par une description, par une peinture: de là procède la longueur ou la brièveté de mes réflexions. (Préface, 65)

This is a claim for freedom in experimenting with stylistic devices. The list of literary *procédés* given above is far from exhaustive. We are well aware, even after a first reading of the *Caractères*, of the extreme variety to be found in La Bruyère's presentation of 'les mœurs de ce siècle'. We may wish that he had been more explicit whenever he comments on his own approach to literary technique, but he has left enough pointers, as we have just seen, for us to realise that he was determined to use all the resources of the literary language of his time, and even to go beyond existing practice if need be, in order to fit in with his own complex, ever-changing vision of the world around him.

In the last passage I mentioned, La Bruyère was mostly concerned with variations in length because at that point in his *Préface* he was stressing the difference between his work and La Rochefoucauld's *Maximes*. But there are other important variations which play as great a part in his creation of an original style, and one of the most interesting aspects of his art is very closely connected with the range of his vocabulary.

Words certainly hold a strong attraction for him. We saw how he regretted the passing of some terms which were becoming obsolete. Did he envy the raciness which French had had in previous centuries? Twice in his book he resorted to the 'vieux langage'. His pastiche of Montaigne has a particular interest not so much in itself as in the impulsion which makes La Bruyère shift from one mode of expression to another:

Je n'aime pas un homme que je ne puis aborder le premier, ni saluer avant qu'il me salue, sans m'avilir à ses yeux, et sans tremper dans la bonne opinion qu'il a de lui-même. MONTAIGNE dirait *'je veux avoir mes coudées franches, et estre courtois et affable ò mon point, sans remords ne conséquence. Je ne puis du tout estriver contre mon penchant,...'* ('De la Société', 30)

This is not a coquettish display of erudite skill. Having stated his dislike of sycophantic behaviour La Bruyère feels the need for a stronger and more striking way of expressing an attitude which is very much part of himself. And who emphasised more than Montaigne with his 'âme toute sienne' that refusal to imitate the courtier's servility of manner? Who better than he coined the style which could express both forcefully and naturally where he stood and why? Thus the affinity La Bruyère perceives between his mood and Montaigne brings with it, one might almost say, the sound of a voice, at least a familiar linguistic pattern which at that instant seems the ideal medium for rendering his thoughts.

Such borrowings, however congenial, remain isolated instances; a passing revelation of moments of close intimacy
between two minds. It is not by resorting to archaisms that La
Bruyère will solve his stylistic problems.

Let us first note that he is perfectly at ease when using the
abstract diction of the classicists, the kind of language which
provides the moralist with handy labels when he wants to
impose on *l'âme humaine* an orderly pattern of definition,
classification and evaluation:

Les vices partent d'une dépravation du cœur; les défauts, d'un vice
de tempérament; le ridicule, d'un défaut d'esprit. ('Des Jugements',
47)

The pattern here is remarkably tidy and achieved with great
economy. The repetition of the words 'vice' and 'défaut'
tightens the connexion between the three different shortcomings in human nature while preserving the distinctions
which La Bruyère is attempting to draw. The meaning of the
two words undergoes a slight alteration as they are first used
in the absolute, and then limited to a much narrower connotation, in a sort of downward movement which parallels
the descending scale 'vice – défaut – ridicule'. The descending
order conveys of course a judgement of value which assesses
the degree of moral responsibility borne respectively by man's
sensibility, his temperament, and his intellectual faculties.

We saw, when examining La Rochefoucauld's long passage
on *amour-propre*, how the art of the classicist can replace a
static definition by a dynamic description and, with exquisite
balance, move along an ambiguous frontier which scarcely
separates the abstract from the concrete, the general concept
from the personification. La Bruyère, more than once, uses
a very similar technique, as, for instance, in his picture of true
greatness as opposed to false greatness:

La véritable grandeur est libre, douce, familière, populaire; elle se
laisse toucher et manier, elle ne perd rien à être vue de près; plus
on la connaît, plus on l'admire. Elle se courbe par bonté vers ses
inférieurs, et revient sans effort dans son naturel; elle s'abandonne

quelquefois, se néglige, se relâche de ses avantages, toujours en pouvoir de les reprendre et de les faire valoir; elle rit, joue et badine, mais avec dignité; on l'approche tout ensemble avec liberté et avec retenue... ('Du Mérite Personnel', 42)

In order to bring out the quintessence of that 'véritable grandeur', La Bruyère depicts it in turn as the possessor of pleasant qualities, as something which can be touched, handled and examined closely, as gestures, as behaviour. Each implied comparison, each suggestion of a physical attitude, is immediately checked by what follows, so that we are left with a harmonious blend of characteristics, and, although never allowed a concrete representation, with the impression of a living presence.

But concrete representation was also something which attracted La Bruyère, not perhaps in itself but as implied in his composition of 'les mœurs de ce siècle', that frieze depicting the civilisation of his age. Was he inspired by the literary tradition which in his century had been the only refuge of the concrete: the tradition of the so-called 'realist' novels, of the burlesque, of certain satiric poems, from Regnier's 'Macette' to Boileau's masterpiece of the genre 'Le Repas Ridicule'? I very much doubt it.

That way of approaching the concrete side of reality tended towards a farcical, debasing picture of men and things. There is no trace of this kind of caricatural exaggeration in the *Caractères*. Look, for instance, at the well-known twin portraits of the rich man and the poor man ('Des Biens de Fortune', 83). A careful selection of physical characteristics, of attitudes, of mannerisms and general behaviour shows in, so to speak, quintessential form how wealth has moulded one man and poverty the other. The portrait is pencilled without any gross distortion of features, any thickening of the outlines. This is stylisation, not caricature.

On the other hand, the influence of Theophrastus may appear more relevant. It is true that in his 'Discours sur Théophraste' La Bruyère tells us that whereas the Greek writer started his study of man's weaknesses from the ex-

ternal evidence of behaviour, he himself had put the stress
on the analysis of the inner man:

L'on s'est plus appliqué aux vices de l'esprit, aux replis du cœur
et à tout l'intérieur de l'homme que n'a fait Théophraste...

It is difficult however to believe that he had remained indifferent to the concrete details of contemporary life in Athens
which Theophrastus had scattered through his book. In fact,
La Bruyère's footnotes to his translation show his interest in
the Athenian ways of eating, drinking, bathing, dressing, in
the forms of entertainment or the religious customs. Even if
these notes are there primarily to help the reader with the
meaning of the text, their minute precision suggests, on the
part of the translator, a pleasurable familiarity with the local
colour of a Greek town. Thus he tells us that marjoram was
useful in the house as it prevented meat from going bad, as
did also thyme and laurel; or that chalk was incorporated in
the making of cheap woollen fabric. We shall find again in La
Bruyère's own *Caractères* this concern for the technical aspect
of a civilisation.

Whether or not Theophrastus was a decisive influence,
the fact remains that the concrete element was to play an
important part in the book. And this is where the freedom La
Bruyère claims to adapt his style to various moods will open
a rich field of experimentation with words. We must also
remember at this point how his *moi* tends at times to come to
the surface of his text. The large space which separates an
abstract statement from a concrete observation gives plenty of
room for such moves and enables the author to shift his
viewpoint, to come closer to his topic or to remain distant, to
intervene in a dialogue or to stand apart.

The world about him

It has been said, and quite rightly, that La Bruyère is a man
'pour qui le monde extérieur existe'.[1] We have already seen

[1] Particularly by Jules Brody in his very fine article 'Sur le style de La Bruyère' in
L'Esprit Créateur, Vol. II, No. 2, Summer, 1971, p. 167.

how he suggests the influence of the physical world on the reactions of our sensibility: the congenial atmosphere of a place, the entrancing sound of a voice, the pleasurable message conveyed by an exchange of looks,[1] This contact with the concrete world around him is even more obvious when he is concerned with what represents the civilisation of his age.

As I said previously, the civilisation of a given period is inseparable from a number of material things: clothes for instance:

Un homme à la cour, et souvent à la ville, qui a un long manteau de soie ou de drap de Hollande, une ceinture large et placée haut sur l'estomac, le soulier de maroquin, la calotte de même, d'un beau grain, un collet bien fait et empesé... ('Du Mérite Personnel', 28)

That was the way a fashionable divine was dressed. With the same precision, La Bruyère mentions a dandy's tall hat, his doublet with puffs on the shoulders, his jackboots and his breeches festooned with ribbons or tags ('De la Mode', 11).

Cvilisation also comprises what the gourmet eats: game and truffles ('Des Femmes', 75); the kind of wine he drinks: 'vins d'Avenay ou de Sillery' ('Des Biens de Fortune', 18); and whereas the rich man gets drunk on the best champagne, the common people fall back on inferior wine from Brie ('Des Grands', 28). Civilisation includes the entertainments which attract Parisians: fireworks, mock tilting matches, military reviews, hunting parties on the day of Saint Hubert, public executions ('De la Ville', 13), fashionable singers (ibid.), and even fashionable quacks ('De Quelques Usages', 68), features of domestic architecture: terraces, gilded ceilings and hot-houses for growing orange trees ('Des Grands', 4).

Such precise details abound in the *Caractères*. It is not enough for La Bruyère to tell us of a house that a man is having built for himself; the solid reality of the house both for the satisfaction of its future owner and for its survival in the book is made safer by the inclusion of iron cramps:

Il fait bâtir dans la rue une maison de pierre de taille, raffermie dans les encoignures par des mains de fer...('De l'Homme', 124)

[1] See Chapter 2, pp. 115–16.

The use of the technical word, which increases considerably the range of La Bruyère's vocabulary, recurs in several places. The author seems to suggest that the immediate reality of the world around us can be seized only through the precise accurate language which labels its components:

On s'élève à la ville dans une indifférence grossière des choses rurales et champêtres; on distingue à peine la plante qui porte le chanvre d'avec celle qui produit le lin,...Ne parlez pas à un grand nombre de bourgeois ni de guérets, ni de baliveaux, ni de provins, ni de regains, si vous voulez être entendu; ces termes pour eux ne sont pas français. ('De la Ville', 21)

If for such men the word which refers to the layering of vines (*provins*) or to the selective clearing of trees in a forest (*baliveaux*) is meaningless, on the other hand they are themselves wrapped up in a network of other technical words which correspond to their own preoccupations: legal jargon (ibid.), terms of heraldry ('De la Ville', 10, 'De Certains Usages', 5) or of hunting (ibid., 11). Thus men perceive only a small part of the world and conversely the personality of each of them is largely constituted by the specialised language he knows and uses.

There is another interesting side to La Bruyère's fondness for the technical aspects of the everyday life of his time. We notice that together with the various categories of people who are being satirised – noblemen, preachers, tax collectors, dandies – there is another group of men whose presence in the work has nothing to do with satire: the craftsmen. They are particularised: the joiner, the tiler, the mason, the carpenter, the sawyer of marble, and so are their tools. They are essentially technicians, and their neutral but eminently respectable quality is that they are nothing more and nothing less than the craft they practise:

...le couvreur songe à couvrir:... ('Du Mérite Personnel', 16)

and they have an exact knowledge of what is required in their task. The artisan knows very well that one does not saw with a plane, nor plane with a saw (Ibid., 8).

These men stand for the genuine form of activity in society, for an objective reality which cannot be denied, as opposed for instance to the fanciful profession of the self-appointed wit:

Je nomme *Eurypyle*, et vous dites: 'C'est un bel esprit'. Vous dites aussi de celui qui travaille une poutre: 'Il est charpentier'; et de celui qui refait un mur: 'Il est maçon'. Je vous demande quel est l'atelier où travaille cet homme de métier, ce bel esprit? quelle est son enseigne? à quel habit le reconnaît-on? quels sont ses outils? est-ce le coin, sont-ce le marteau ou l'enclume? où fend-il, ou cogne-t-il son ouvrage? ('Des Jugements', 20)

Incidentally this is why La Bruyère as a writer considers himself one of these technicians. Making a book is as much of a craft as making a clock. He underlines the technicality of the tools of his trade:

Qu'on ne me parle jamais d'encre, de papier, de plume, de style, d'imprimeur, d'imprimerie... ('Des Jugements', 21)

and considers that he should be paid for his books as the tiler is paid for his tiles (ibid.).

I have used the expression 'objective reality'. We might be tempted to see in La Bruyère's use of concrete and technical detail a form of realism. But we must be careful not to let ourselves be carried away by an anachronistic point of view nor to judge La Bruyère according to what we know of realism in the nineteenth or twentieth centuries. There is no systematic attempt in the *Caractères* to copy the physical reality of the world or to render the local colour of seventeenth-century France. The concrete element sometimes appears and sometimes not. It is carefully dispensed, always stylised, and never used for its own sake.

But as we read the book, a certain number of objects are conjured up, as they must have been at the time. One inevitably thinks of the well-known passage on the coach:

Une femme de ville entend-elle le bruissement d'un carrosse qui s'arrête à sa porte, elle pétille de goût et de complaisance pour quiconque est dedans, sans le connaître; mais si elle a vu de sa

fenêtre un bel attelage, beaucoup de livrées, et que plusieurs rangs
de clous parfaitement dorés l'aient ébloui, quelle impatience n'a-t-elle
pas de voir déjà dans sa chambre le cavalier ou le magistrat! quelle
charmante réception ne lui fera-t-elle point!...on lui tient compte
des doubles soupentes et des ressorts qui le font rouler plus molle-
ment... ('De la Ville', 15)

The coach is of course used as an illustration of the snobbery
of the Parisian lady who feels a great esteem for whoever
possesses such a superb carriage. But we can hear the kind
of noise the coach makes when it stops at the door, we can
feel its comfortable springs and see its gleaming golden studs,
beautifully polished.

Even more immediately present and alive are the tulips in
the famous passage of the *fleuriste*:

...Vous le voyez planté, et qui a pris racine au milieu de ses tulipes
et devant la *Solitaire*; il ouvre de grands yeux, il frotte ses mains, il
se baisse, il la voit de plus près, il ne l'a jamais vue si belle, il a le cœur
épanoui de joie; il la quitte pour l'*Orientale*, de là il va à la *Veuve*,
il passe au *Drap d'or*, de celle-ci à l'*Agathe*, d'où il revient enfin à la
Solitaire, où il se fixe, où il se lasse, où il s'assit, où il oublie de dîner:
aussi est-elle nuancée, bordée, huilée, à pièces emportées; elle a un
beau vase ou un beau calice... ('De la Mode', 2)

Here again, the tulips are an illustration of a human folly.
The man grows tulips only because tulips are the fashion; but
at the same time La Bruyère has caught and fixed the
entrancing reality of a beautiful tulip, particularly the glisten-
ing of the petals. He has also conveyed the almost magical
attraction contained in the name of a flower: *l'Orientale, le Drap
d'or*. These very names are in themselves, to the gardener, a
promise of splendour just as nowadays such names as Mer-
maid or Super Star set afire the imagination of the rose-grower.

Most of the time the concrete element is used, as we have
seen, to illustrate a particular moral shortcoming. But the
number of illustrations suggests a very close connexion between the workings of man's mind and the material world
around him. That connexion certainly did not escape the
insight of a moralist like La Rochefoucauld and we have seen

149

how well he was aware, for instance, of the physical conditioning of man; however, what interested him was the consequence of the connexion, the kind of determinism it imposed on man's reactions rather than the connexion itself, whereas La Bruyère seems to be fascinated at times by the exact point where a mental reaction meets the physical world.

For instance, La Rochefoucauld might have said that some of our so-called feelings are easily forgotten in favour of insignificant matters. Here is the way La Bruyère puts it:

Il ne faut quelquefois qu'une jolie maison dont on hérite, qu'un beau cheval ou un joli chien dont on se trouve le maître, qu'une tapisserie, qu'une pendule, pour adoucir une grande douleur, et pour faire moins sentir une grande perte. ('De l'Homme', 31)

The part played on our mind by material objects, the ludicrous lack of hierarchy in our sense of values, are given here a remarkable emphasis. The 'grande douleur' sounds dull, abstract, removed, coming after a string of precise concrete objects which seem to become brighter and more tangible as they decrease in size and importance: 'Une jolie maison', 'un beau cheval', 'un joli chien', 'une tapisserie', 'une pendule'. The tapestry and the clock stand out in astonishing relief.

The moralist is fully justified, as a moralist, in making this type of remark: it is part of his study of human nature. Men's feelings and thoughts naturally move along the surface of reality. Just as a man's personality is both revealed and circumscribed by the kind of vocabulary he uses, so it is shaped by the concrete world around him.

This La Bruyère has amply illustrated but, in both cases, by doing so he has moved from a general feature of mankind to the individual reaction, a change in his angle of vision. With each of such illustrations we are no longer concerned with fundamental characteristics but with a single experience, unique of its kind, springing to life with the vivid colours of its immediacy and also subjected to the limitations of an idiosyncracy. This shift from the general to the idiosyncratic can be observed in many places in the *Caractères*. There is a

particularly striking example in the section 'De l'Homme',
(144).

At the beginning of the paragraph La Bruyère describes and
analyses in general terms what he calls 'la fausse délicatesse',
that is, the desire in some people to appear to possess a finer
sensibility than anybody else. He then goes on:

> La fausse délicatesse de goût et de complexion n'est telle...que
> parce qu'elle est feinte ou affectée: c'est *Emilie* qui crie de toute
> sa force sur un petit péril qui ne lui fait pas peur; c'est une autre
> qui par mignardise pâlit à la vue d'une souris, ou qui veut aimer les
> violettes et s'évanouir aux tubéreuses.

The camera has moved. The final close-up leaves us un-
expectedly, and pleasurably too, with the concrete reality of
fragrant violets and tuberoses. The shift from general considerations to a concrete fact may take place without transition
and be a sudden transposition into another key, a deliberate
play on dissonances, as in the following passage, where we are
brought down with a jerk from major abstract considerations
on the behaviour of a wise man to a very minor everyday
occurrence:

> L'homme du meilleur esprit est inégal; il souffre des accroissements
> et des diminutions, il entre en verve, mais il en sort; alors, s'il est sage,
> il parle peu, il n'écrit point, il ne cherche point à imaginer ni à plaire.
> Chante-t-on avec un rhume?... ('De l'Homme', 142)

La Bruyère is certainly very conscious, as an artist, of the
value, either humourous or poetic, or both, of these sudden
glimpses of the concrete reality of the universe and of the
details of ordinary existence.

IMAGINATION

Given La Bruyère's wish to bring together abstract and concrete elements, it is hardly surprising that his choice of metaphors and similes should offer some interesting features.

We ought perhaps to remember at this point that for the
seventeenth century, as for the sixteenth, imagination was not

a quality to be appreciated unreservedly, and La Bruyère voices the traditional mistrust:

Il ne faut pas qu'il y ait trop d'imagination dans nos conversations ni dans nos écrits; elle ne produit souvent que des idées vaines et puériles, qui ne servent point à perfectionner le goût et à nous rendre meilleurs... ('De la Société', 17)

On the other hand, his strong impulse to innovate in matters of images as elsewhere prompts him to state that:

...l'on peut...en une sorte d'écrits hasarder de certaines expressions, user de termes transposés et qui peignent vivement, et plaindre ceux qui ne sentent pas le plaisir qu'il y a à s'en servir ou à les entendre. ('Des Ouvrages de l'Esprit', 66)

His practice is much more in keeping with this second pronouncement than with the first, and he is in this respect very different from La Rochefoucauld.

In the *Maximes*, as we have seen, the metaphors were unobtrusive and on the whole deliberately unoriginal. La Rochefoucauld conforms to the classicist's esthetics and never allows a personal flight of fancy to upset the delicate balance of a maxim. La Bruyère at times abides by the same esthetic principles:

La cour est comme un édifice bâti de marbre: je veux dire qu'elle est composée d'hommes fort durs, mais fort polis. ('De la Cour', 10)

The 'marbre' image is traditional; its aptness acquires a particular force as it stands for two characteristics instead of just one. Wit depends on the coupling of these two qualities – hardness of heart and civilised polish – and not on the picturesqueness of the metaphor chosen.

But very often, on the contrary, the effect of La Bruyère's metaphor depends on an original twist given to the traditional image. This is how he characterises some courtiers:

...ils n'ont pas, si je l'ose dire, deux pouces de profondeur; si vous les enfoncez, vous rencontrez le tuf. ('De la Cour', 83)

To set mental shallowness alongside physical shallowness is in itself a well-acknowledged comparison but here very much modified by the precision given to depth – two inches – by the concrete movement – 'si vous les enfoncez' – and by the unexpected mention of an almost technical term 'le tuf' (sub-soil). This is in fact the deliberate elaboration and extension of an outworn image in order to give it back its evocative power.

In the same way, La Bruyère's occasional use of a traditional simile reveals his desire to infuse new life into it or to present it with fresh colouring:

L'on voit *Eustrate* assis dans sa nacelle, où il jouit d'un air pur et d'un ciel serein: il avance d'un bon vent et qui a toutes les apparences de devoir durer; mais il tombe tout d'un coup, le ciel se couvre, l'orage se déclare, un tourbillon enveloppe la nacelle, elle est submergée: on voit Eustrate revenir sur l'eau et faire quelques efforts; on espère qu'il pourra du moins se sauver et venir à bord; mais une vague l'enfonce, on le tient perdu; il paraît une seconde fois, et les espérances se réveillent, lorsqu'un flot survient et l'abîme; on ne le revoit plus, il est noyé. ('De la Mode', 9)

The sea voyage, storm and shipwreck which stand for Eustrate's ambitious hopes, struggles and final social disaster take the form of a lively narrative. The rapidity of the dramatic action, its small scale which precludes any tragic emotion (the anti-tragic note being struck from the very beginning by the mention of the diminutive boat without mast or sail which no one in his senses would trust), the fact that the adventure is presented so to speak laterally, through the reactions of the spectators watching it ('on voit', 'on espère', 'on le tient perdu'. . .) denote an extremely skilful technique. The age-long simile has been enlivened by a process of acceleration and terseness. A touch of immediacy has been added which combines paradoxically with an impression of total unreality as we are reminded all the time of the ironically sympathetic spectators who are contemplating his progress not in seafaring but in social life.

Equally significant is the treatment of another traditional simile: the shepherd and his flock, representing the ruler and his people:

6-2

Quand vous voyez quelquefois un nombreux troupeau, qui répandu sur une colline vers le déclin d'un beau jour, paît tranquillement le thym et le serpolet, ou qui broute dans une prairie une herbe menue et tendre qui a échappé à la faux du moissonneur, le berger, soigneux et attentif, est debout auprès de ses brebis; il ne les perd pas de vue, il les suit, il les conduit, il les change de pâturage; si elles se dispersent, il les rassemble; si un loup avide paraît, il lâche son chien qui le met en fuite;... Image naïve des peuples et du prince qui les gouverne, s'il est bon prince.

Le faste et le luxe dans un souverain, c'est le berger habillé d'or et de pierreries, la houlette d'or en ses mains; son chien a un collier d'or, il est attaché avec une laisse d'or et de soie. Que sert tant d'or à son troupeau ou contre les loups? ('Du Souverain', 29)

Here we have a slowing down of the tempo, with La Bruyère lingering over the charm of a naïve pastoral setting (beautiful evening, wild thyme and tender grass, succulent pastures) and the activities of the ever-watchful shepherd. This is already a decorative elaboration of a traditional scene. The contrasting picture of the sheep-dog with a gold collar and silk leash following his bejewelled master modifies even further the original simile, adding to the classical tableau the heavy gilding of rococo embellishments.

Most of the time, however, La Bruyère shows a strong preference for the non-literary metaphor. The connexion provided by the metaphor is no longer with a tradition which gives imagery the gloss of a patina, but with the everyday world which surrounds the writer.

Hence the comparison of the man of letters with a clock-maker ('Des Ouvrages de l'Esprit', 3), of the courtier with a watch ('De la Cour', 65), of court life with a game of draughts (ibid. 64), of the man who is known by everybody with the verger of the parish church, or with 'le saint de pierre qui orne le grand autel' ('De l'Homme', 125). La Bruyère's liking for this kind of metaphor can be seen throughout the book. He seems to take a special delight in coming on some unexpected connexion between a mental feature and the concrete world and in creating stimulating patterns out of such *rapprochements*.

Because La Bruyère uses so many material details taken from contemporary life, most critics have admired his gift of observation. I would praise his quality of imagination and see him not as an observer but as a poet.

Like a poet he feels the need to translate into another key, and sometimes into several keys, the human reality he considers. This is, for instance, how he characterises the atmosphere created by the social mixture round the gambling tables:

...c'est comme une musique qui détonne; ce sont comme des couleurs mal assorties, comme des paroles qui jurent et qui offensent l'oreille,.... ('Des Biens de Fortune', 71)

trying in turn, for an accurate comparison, the fields of music, colours and diction.

This is also what often gives to his illustrations an amusing touch of fancy. At one point in the chapter 'Des Jugements' he is concerned with the kind of people who are gifted only at one thing and who apart from that particular gift are stupid or at least boring. A common experience, which La Rochefoucauld had expressed in a general form:

On ne plaît pas longtemps quand on n'a que d'une sorte d'esprit. (413)

La Bruyère illustrates the fact with various examples and, among others:

...un musicien par exemple, qui après m'avoir comme enchanté par ses accords, semble s'être remis avec son luth dans un même étui,... ('Des Jugements', 56)

We witness the leap into the world of fantasy – the ludicrous picture of the man disappearing into the case with the instrument – and we enjoy the pleasurable effect of this poetic quirk.

The same flight of imagination prompts La Bruyère to visualise the so-called castle of a would-be nobleman as:

...une ruine qui trempe dans un marécage,... ('De Quelques Usages', 6) or, when describing the activities of the man intent on making money, to note that such a man would with savage energy draw gold from what is normally free:

...il exigera un droit de tous ceux qui boivent de l'eau de la rivière, ou qui marchent sur la terre ferme... ('Des Biens de Fortune', 28)

and out of the most improbable things:

...il sait convertir en or jusqu'aux roseaux, aux joncs et à l'ortie. (Ibid.)

Note here again the unexpected close-up, the sudden focussing on the vision of a piece of land overgrown with reeds, rushes and nettles.

It is clear, I think, from these last examples that La Bruyère's imagination plays with concrete elements in many different ways, and with such flexibility that one would often hesitate to use any of the conventional terms of rhetoric, including the word metaphor, to qualify the picture he conjures up in the mind.

In the following sentence:

Le comédien couché dans son carrosse jette de la boue au visage de CORNEILLE qui est à pied. ('Des Jugements', 17)

should we take the scene literally (as an imaginary but possible happening) or metaphorically? The implications are the same in both cases – society does not reward men of letters – and our hesitation in fact intensifies the impact of the illustration. And also it seems that La Bruyère has stretched the ambiguous frontier which separates abstraction from concreteness, making it into a kind of no-man's land where surprising alliances of terms take place.

L'on se couche à la cour et l'on se lève sur l'intérêt; c'est ce que l'on digère le matin et le soir, le jour et la nuit... ('De la Cour', 22)

The effect of these lines depends on a complex interaction of the expressions used; the bold construction 'se lever sur l'intérêt' is made possible by its being coupled with the more usual 'se coucher sur', while retaining its originality. 'Digérer', because it is made part of a natural rhythm of daily life – going to bed, getting up, etc. – recaptures part of its physiological import without losing its suggestion of a mental obsession.[1]

When we see the vastness and difficulty of mapping the *domaine de l'imaginaire* in the *Caractères*, we are strongly tempted to think that, as far as the concrete world is concerned, there is not to be found here a clear-cut difference between illustrations and metaphors. The objects La Bruyère mentions – flowers, animals, plants, pieces of furniture, instruments, carriages, ornaments, etc. – no longer belong to the everyday reality around him. They have been turned into symbols. Out of the material world, out of the civilisation of his time, La Bruyère has created a sort of poetic universe which corresponds to his own vision of things and men. When we come across a poet's personal vision we realise that, whatever elements the writer has taken from external reality, they have been selected, stylised and rearranged according to an individual pattern. Most poets have their favourite motifs. We cannot conceive Nerval's world without the star, Shelley's landscape otherwise than delicately blurred by a constant shimmering, nor Byron's poetic world without the sea. The dominant pattern in the *Caractères* is the pattern of movement. It is perfectly understandable that it should be so, as La Bruyère is concerned with catching the most fleeting, the most elusive aspects of man through man's seventeenth-century avatar. Since he is the poet of the ephemeral, he will be the poet of motion.

When we read the *Caractères* we meet a great many people either as individuals or as groups of men but we almost never see their faces or their figures; we see their movements.

Here is Cydias, the *bel esprit*:

...Cydias, après avoir toussé, relevé sa manchette, étendu la main et ouvert les doigts... ('De la Société', 75)

and Troïle, the all-powerful favourite of his master:

---

[1] André Stegman, commenting on this remark, puts it more succinctly: '...plutôt que des figures, ce sont des associations insolites qui donnent un tour métaphorique à l'expression'. (Op. cit., p. 150)

Si l'on entre par malheur sans avoir une physionomie qui lui agrée, il ride son front et il détourne sa vue; si on l'aborde, il ne se lève pas; si l'on s'assied auprès de lui, il s'éloigne; si on lui parle, il ne répond point; si l'on continue de parler, il passe dans une autre chambre; si on le suit, il gagne l'escalier... (Ibid., 13)

References to movements are also found in comparisons. This is how La Bruyère ridicules those men of very average merit who ape the modest countenance of the truly great men:

...[ils] contrefont les simples et les naturels: semblables à ces gens d'une taille médiocre qui se baissent aux portes, de peur de se heurter. ('Du Mérite Personnel', 17)[1]

Movements become violent when La Bruyère's satire is at its more virulent and when he finds a vice particularly repulsive. The monstrosity of Gnathon's selfishness is exposed through the man's abominable table manners and animal-like frantic voracity:

...il ne se sert à table que de ses mains; il manie les viandes, les remanie, démembre, déchire... ('De l'Homme', 121)

And we remember too La Bruyère's metaphorical attack on the courtiers: 'pressez-les, tordez-les...'.[2]

The result of such focussing on people's movements is that we have at times the same impression as if we were watching a silent film without the captions. In the chapter 'De la Ville' we see the Parisians walking up and down the Cours la Reine, or in the Tuileries, or along the Seine, at the time when it is the right thing to be there (for places, avenues and streets are ephemeral too, like everything else):

...l'on gesticule et l'on badine, l'on penche négligemment la tête, l'on passe et l'on repasse. (3)

We see:

...un peuple qui cause, bourdonne, parle à l'oreille, éclate de rire... (4)

---

[1] There is a curious reminiscence of La Bruyère in Balzac: 'Lucien aurait bien voulu se glisser dans le salon, à la manière des gens célèbres qui, par une fausse modestie, se baisseraient sous la porte Saint-Denis.' (*Les Illusions Perdues*, IIIe partie)

[2] See Chapter 2, p. 122–3.

We shall never know what makes them laugh or what secrets they whisper. These men and women are like moving shadows on a wall; none of the rest of their individuality is mentioned. La Bruyère's characters often seem to be movement and nothing else, so that we wonder what provokes the movement, or even if there is any reason for it. We watch those who haunt the house of an important personage:

... ils montent l'escalier d'un ministre, et ils en descendent; ils sortent de son antichambre, et ils y rentrent. ('De la Cour', 61)

until the acceleration of speed gives the unremitting mobility of some courtiers the appearance of maniacal restlessness:

On ne les a jamais vus assis, jamais fixes et arrêtés; qui même les a vus marcher? on les voit courir, parler en courant, et vous interroger sans attendre de réponse. Ils ne viennent d'aucun endroit, ils ne vont nulle part; ils passent et ils repassent. (Ibid., 19)

People in the *Caractères* seem to be endlessly going up and down stairs, opening and shutting doors, leaning out of windows, coming into houses and going out.

It is not therefore surprising that when La Bruyère considers to what length the inventiveness of a man interested only in his own comfort can go his imagination leaps over centuries and foresees both the lift and the electric eye:

Il faisait dix pas pour aller de son lit dans sa garde-robe, il n'en fait plus que neuf par la manière dont il a su tourner sa chambre: combien de pas épargnés dans le cours d'une vie! Ailleurs on tourne la clef, l'on pousse contre, ou l'on tire à soi, et une porte s'ouvre: quelle fatigue! voilà un mouvement de trop, qu'il sait s'épargner, et comment? c'est un mystère qu'il ne révèle point; ... Hermippe tire le jour de son appartement d'ailleurs que de la fenêtre; il a trouvé le secret de monter et de descendre autrement que par l'escalier, et il cherche celui d'entrer et de sortir plus commodément que par la porte. ('De Quelques Usages', 64)

Such is La Bruyère's obsession with movement that he fancies to himself men in the most influential positions, and therefore most dangerously placed, being carried away in a kind of infernal whirling dance which ends in a disaster as dazzling and as spectacular as fireworks:

Il ne sont jamais que sur un pied; mobiles comme le mercure, ils pirouettent, ils gesticulent, ils crient, ils s'agitent; semblables à ces figures de carton qui servent de montre à une fête publique, ils jettent feu et flamme, tonnent et foudroient...jusques à ce que, venant à s'éteindre, ils tombent... ('Des Grands', 32)

If movement, thus stylised, is an important element in the creation of a poetic world it is often at the same time a source of comedy. Mechanical movements are comic, and more than once in the book human behaviour assumes the regular pattern of an absurd *va-et-vient*. Here is, for instance, the comic pattern which ridicules the tight relations between 'dévot' and 'dévotes':

...elles vont, et il va; elles reviennent, et il revient; elles demeurent, et il demeure... ('De la Mode', 24)

The comic touch is always applied with deftness so that it blends happily with the nuances of either an abstract judgement or an imaginary picture. Comedy in the *Caractères* never verges on caricature, and, although relying a great deal on the concrete, has a marked 'intellectual' quality which we shall find again.

This poetic and humourous vision of men and things is as far from a realistic approach to contemporary life as possible. Its own arbitrary dimensions and dynamic patterns are mercifully free from the constraints of *vraisemblance*. This enables La Bruyère to shake the reader's normal picture of the world and to give to the most hyperbolical statements an uncanny sense of immediacy as, for instance, in the following 'impossible' dialogue:

Fuyez, retirez-vous: vous n'êtes pas assez loin. – Je suis, dites-vous, sous l'autre tropique. – Passez sous le pôle et dans l'autre hémisphère; montez aux étoiles, si vous les pouvez. – M'y voilà. – Fort bien, vous êtes en sureté. ('Des Biens de Fortune', 35)

It is because with La Bruyère the imaginative faculty is always ready to take advantage of a promising topic that, however much he may disapprove of human follies, some of them afford him the most pleasurable speculations, and the intellectual quality of his comic vision becomes then particularly marked.

Absent-mindedness is a common foible, but how far will the absent-minded man go, when acting according to the mechanism of absent-mindedness once the latter is wound up? Hence the long development of the well-known portrait of Ménalque, the 'distrait' ('De l'Homme', 7).

This technique of testing the mechanism until it reaches the point of absurdity and breaks down is at its best in the portrait of Diphile, 'l'amateur d'oiseaux':

Diphile commence par un oiseau et finit par mille; sa maison n'en est pas égayée mais empestée: la cour, la salle, l'escalier, le vestibule, les chambres, le cabinet, tout est volière... ('De la Mode', 2)

La Bruyère enumerates the various activities of Diphile: 'il passe les jours, ces jours qui échappent et qui ne reviennent plus', (note here the recurrent obsession with the passage of time) 'à verser du grain et à nettoyer des ordures'.

The passage ends with a superb crescendo which is the sheer intellectual and esthetic pleasure of reaching the improbable climax within the framework of logical deduction:

...il retrouve ses oiseaux dans son sommeil: lui-même il est oiseau, il est huppé, il gazouille, il perche; il rêve la nuit qu'il mue, ou qu'il couve.

It is perhaps relatively easy for one of La Bruyère's characters to undergo such a metamorphosis, for in this universe where concrete elements are so important, where material objects stand out in remarkable relief, the physical reality of human beings is very elusive. The golden studs of the coach shine brightly, the petals of the tulips glisten, houses stand solidly, firmly secured by iron clamps, but where is the man or the woman? A mouth opens but there is no face. We see a hand stretching from under a cuff and the fingers move. We witness a nod, a frown, a bow, nothing more. It seems that man, even more ephemeral than all the rest, dissolves in the very movements which are his *raison d'être*.

Here is one more typical instance. There could be a hundred others:

D'où vient qu'Alcippe me salue aujourd'hui, me sourit, et se jette hors d'une portière de peur de me manquer? Je ne suis pas riche et je suis à pied... ('De l'Homme ', 74)

We are told only of the gestures and movements of the protagonists in this little scene. Alcippe's smile is the smile of the Cheshire cat.

La Bruyère is famous for his portraits. Are they, paradoxically, portraits of invisible men? We think we have caught a man, but we are left with a shoe or a doublet, a collection of etchings or a necklace. In the portrait of the absent-minded man, an insubstantial Ménalque bumps into solid objects, the shaft of a cart or the work-bench of a joiner.

8

THE CIVILISED MAN

This world of puppets who sit down, get up, come in, go out, smile, shrug their shoulders, open their mouths, push back their cuffs is undoubtedly a satire on La Bruyère's contemporaries.[1] But the full significance of the picture is not limited to the seventeenth century and is closely connected with some of the central preoccupations of the moralist, for it is also a judgement on man and on civilisation in general.

The fool is defined as a mere mechanism:

Le sot est automate, il est machine, il est ressort, le poids l'emporte, le fait mouvoir, le fait tourner, et toujours, et dans le même sens, et avec la même égalité. ('De l'Homme', 142)

All men are not fools, but civilisation imposes on all of them its regular rhythm, its engineered directions and patterns of automatic behaviour. Civilised men live mechanically. They are hollow men, leading empty lives.

Such is the courtier whom La Bruyère compares to a watch with its hidden springs and wheels and the slow movement of its hand which never departs from its circular progress ('De la Cour', 65). And is not the courtier the prototype of the civilised man?

The life of the man about town, Narcisse, is also characterised by its tedious repetition of the same actions, rigidly in keeping with social dictates. He goes regularly to mass in one of the fashionable churches, plays cards in the same place every day at the same time, takes a walk at the right hour of the day along the *Cours la Reine* and pays social calls with the most religious punctuality. La Bruyère starts the portrait by telling us that:

[1] This point is emphasised by J. Brody at the end of his essay on La Bruyère's style. He praises the moralist for having seen in this 'monde chosifié et déspiritualisé' the disintegration of the values nobility stood for and adds: 'Si La Bruyère s'obstinait à peindre ses contemporains par le dehors, c'est tout simplement parce que ses contemporains, surtout nobles, ne lui montraient plus autre chose.' (Op. cit., p. 167)

Narcisse se lève le matin pour se coucher le soir... ('De la Ville', 12)

and ends with the following remark:

Il fera demain ce qu'il fait aujourd'hui et ce qu'il fit hier; et il meurt ainsi après avoir vécu.

A woman's day is regulated by the same, meaningless routine, or a worse one:

...se chercher incessamment les unes et les autres avec l'impatience de ne se point rencontrer; ne se rencontrer que pour se dire des riens, que pour apprendre réciproquement des choses dont on est également instruite,...n'entrer dans une chambre précisément que pour en sortir; ne sortir de chez soi l'après-dînée que pour y rentrer le soir,... ('De la Ville', 20)

Men and women live on the surface of life and they 'have measured out their lives' if not 'with coffee spoons' at least in the number of toys which civilisation provides them with: clothes and coaches, flowers and medals, book-bindings and curios, horses and dogs – all of them telling symbols of fickleness and stultifying frivolity. I say toys, but even the smallest of them may be of immense importance, since people assess one another's values according to purely external evidence, and half an inch of ribbon may be a matter of great concern:

...le monde veut de la parure, on lui en donne; il est avide de la superfluité, on lui en montre.... Il y a des endroits où il faut se faire valoir: un galon d'or plus large ou plus étroit vous fait entrer ou refuser. ('De l'Homme', 71)

What counts is the superficial appearance, the cloak or the tinsel, the mask or the posture. One is inevitably led to think of such a world as a stage.[1] And this impression we have at times, when reading the *Caractères*, of watching short scenes from a play is further reinforced by the recurrent dialogue-pattern which I mentioned previously,[2] by those snatches of

[1] In a perceptive article Michel Guggenheim depicts the world of the *Caractères* as 'ce monde théâtral et clos où chacun se trouve continuellement sous les feux de la rampe' and notes that in such a society 'La primauté du paraître sur l'être se manifeste sans cesse.' ('L'homme sous le regard d'autrui ou le monde de La Bruyère', *P.M.L.A.*, vol. LXXXI, no. 7, Dec., 1960).

[2] See Chapter 5, pp. 108–9.

conversation often made more vividly 'scenic' by the accompanying gestures or mimicries.

As might be expected, La Bruyère's own version of the traditional 'theatre of the world' is strongly influenced by his obsession with time. What depresses him most is the thought that the same puppet-show will repeat itself for years and years, the same patterns of inept movements, the same play with the same decor. Only the actors will vanish, but will easily be replaced by other men ready to play the same parts, as all the actors are in fact sadly interchangeable:

Dans cent ans le monde subsistera encore en son entier: ce sera le même théâtre et les mêmes décorations, ce ne seront plus les mêmes acteurs... tous auront disparu de dessus la scène. Il s'avance déjà sur le théâtre d'autres hommes qui vont jouer dans une même pièce les mêmes rôles; ils s'évanouiront à leur tour; et ceux qui ne sont pas encore, un jour ne seront plus: de nouveaux acteurs ont pris leur place. ('De la Cour', 99)

We must remember at this point that civilisation is guilty of much worse crimes than its tedious conditioning and its ineradicable levity. The destruction of the inner man, the relentless pursuit of what bears the stamp of social success – money or honours – can provoke not a wry smile of amusement but an outburst of indignation.

In the *Caractères*, civilisation, viewed from different angles, assumes different aspects: hard and cruel because of all the social injustices it brings with it, fragile as it is so essentially short-lived, poetic through the network of concrete objects which are its very substance, comic and inept to the point of absurdity. And this is not all. La Bruyère's judgement on society is certainly ambiguous, for if on the one hand the civilised man appears to him both vicious and ridiculous, he is not in favour of a return to nature or even a retreat into solitude. Far from it.

Man is meant to be a sociable being and to live in society as harmoniously as possible; and La Bruyère has no sympathy for the Alcestes of this world and their moods as *atrabilaires*:

Ce qu'on appelle humeur est une chose trop négligée parmi les hommes: ils devraient comprendre qu'il ne leur suffit pas d'être bons, mais qu'ils doivent encore paraître tels, du moins s'ils tendent à être sociables, capables d'union et de commerce, c'est-à-dire à être des hommes. ('De l'Homme', 9)

To judge from these lines, it seems that the outward appearance of benevolence is meant to complement an already existing kindness of heart. But elsewhere La Bruyère states that the appearance is a substitute for a basic quality which remains out of reach. In an interesting passage he refers to those ready-made sentences men use to congratulate one another on a happy event and notes that most of the time they do not imply genuine concern nor affection, nor are they received with gratitude. And yet:

...il n'est pas permis avec cela de les omettre, parce que du moins elles sont l'image de ce qu'il y a au monde de meilleur, qui est l'amitié, et que les hommes, ne pouvant guère compter les uns sur les autres pour la réalité, semblent être convenus entre eux de se contenter des apparences. ('De la Cour', 81)

It is clear, however, that for La Bruyère virtue and politeness do not necessarily go together:

Avec de la vertu, de la capacité, et une bonne conduite, l'on peut être insupportable. ('De la Société', 31)

neither do intelligence and refinement of manners:

La grossièreté, la rusticité, la brutalité peuvent être les vices d'un homme d'esprit. ('Des Jugements', 48)

In this importance attached to urbane behaviour and social elegance we easily recognise the ideal of the *honnête homme* which La Bruyère shares with the other seventeenth-century moralists. But his views on the subject are coloured by his own temperament.

Bad manners are castigated with particular violence, as, for instance, in his portrait of the self-centred noisy bully Théodecte ('De la Société', 12), or in his description of Gnathon's revolting table manners.

He also adds some characteristic nuances to the refinement of manners which may be expected from the *honnête homme*. We have seen La Rochefoucauld's concern for polite, intelligent, enjoyable – in short civilised – conversation,[1] and for a delicate handling of topics which might infringe on the interlocutor's private feelings.[2] La Bruyère also insists on tact, but in a slightly different way and with specific illustrations: do not expatiate on the good meal you have just had in front of people who can scarcely afford their daily bread, nor on your robust health when talking to invalids, and so on ('De la Société', 160).

What is more significant of his own sensibility is the note of warmth which often accompanies his advice:

L'esprit de la conversation consiste bien moins à en montrer beaucoup qu'à en faire trouver aux autres:...et le plaisir le plus délicat est de faire celui d'autrui. ('De la Société', 16)

C'est rusticité que de donner de mauvaise grâce: le plus fort et le plus pénible est de donner; que coûte-t-il d'y ajouter un sourire? ('De la Cour', 45)

This kind of delicacy and grace implies intellectual insight and the desire to please. La Bruyère is well aware that there are also in any code of manners arbitrary rules, finicky points of etiquette easy to follow if you know them but impossible to guess, however intelligent you are. To judge a man by solecisms in that field before he has had time to learn would be, he thinks wrong and unwise ('Des Jugements', 36). An interesting remark, not only because it shows how perceptive and generous La Bruyère can be in his judgements of the men he observes, but because it relates to a kind of hierarchy of values he establishes between the various aspects of what is called politeness.

There is no doubt that for him the highest form of urbanity concerns the mind:

[1] This was part of a long tradition in France and can be seen in Montaigne, particularly in his remarkable chapter 'De l'art de conférer', (*Essais*, III, VIII).
[2] See Chapter 3, p. 72.

Il faut très peu de fonds pour la politesse dans les manières; il en faut beaucoup pour celle de l'esprit ('Des Jugements', 18)

This remark comes after a passage in which La Bruyère, illustrating his point by mentioning contemporary personages of outstanding importance, attacks the common prejudice that a learned man is necessarily devoid of social graces. The men he gives as examples are both 'doctes' and 'polis'. He even suggests that the second quality is the outcome of the first. Here the notion of civilisation becomes very much akin to that of culture. Men like Condé or Vendôme are praised as 'princes qui ont su joindre aux plus belles et aux plus hautes connaissances et l'atticisme des Grecs et l'urbanité des Romains' (ibid.). This is not just flattery. More than once, and particularly in the first chapter 'Des Ouvrages de l'esprit', La Bruyère insists on the value of the cultural heritage.

It is also very clear that for him the supreme refinement of a civilised society is a question of the right esthetic judgement, a question of 'goût':

Il y a dans l'art un point de perfection, comme de bonté ou de maturité dans la nature. Celui qui le sent et qui l'aime a le goût parfait; celui qui ne le sent pas, et qui aime en deça ou au delà, a le goût défectueux. ('Des Ouvrages de l'Esprit', 10)

The importance attached to that almost indefinable quality of refinement implies a sophisticated form of civilisation which makes it possible for men and women to react with fastidious precision in keeping with such an exacting criterion. Conversely, the highest degree of achievement must be expected from the arts of poetry, music, painting, and even oratory. In those fields nothing short of perfection is acceptable (ibid., 7).

La Bruyère's deep concern for art was criticised by Julian Benda as representing a decadent shift of values.[1] He saw the author of the *Caractères* as an artist in words for art's sake, as the man who prefers the artificial to the natural, who expresses the charm of a small town by saying that 'Elle me paraît peinte sur le penchant d'une colline' ('De la Société', 49).

[1] 'Vous me semblez le père de notre byzantinisme' (op. cit., p. 184).

Ainsi le première idée qui vous vient, pour exprimer que cette chose est aimable, c'est qu'elle vous paraît *peinte*, qu'elle vous paraît un produit de l'art! Les autres trouvent l'art admirable pour autant qu'il évoque la réalité. Vous, vous goûtez la réalité pour ce qu'elle ressemble à l'art. Vous êtes de ceux qui aiment les fruits dans la mesure où ils rappellent les confitures.[1]

This is a somewhat distorted view of La Bruyère's approach to the ideal of naturalness ('Combien d'art pour rentrer dans la nature!....). Yet however unfairly Benda presses his arguments,[2] it is probable that La Bruyère, in his search for a new kind of artistic perfection, was at times very near to upsetting the relations between life and art, truth and art, which had been those of the Renaissance and of classicism. We have seen how conscious he was of coming 'trop tard', but whether the originality of his frequent departures from an exhausted literary tradition and his wish to put into his writings 'une finesse de tour, et quelquefois une trop grande délicatesse' ('Des Ouvrages de l'Esprit', 57) were symptomatic of a near-Byzantine civilisation is a very debatable point.

Fastidious esthetic tastes may seem a long way from impeccable table manners, but civilisation, as reflected in the *Caractères*, has many facets. Its value remains ambiguous. Its elegance, even its more solid intellectual qualities, are seen as a thin varnish:

...celui qui n'a vu que des hommes polis et raisonnables, ou ne connaît pas l'homme, ou ne le connaît qu'à demi;... ('De l'Homme', 156)

Good breeding colours men with a uniform dye which masks the most unpleasant idiosyncrasies of human nature as well as their appalling number and variety. One needs only to observe the common people or the provincials (civilisation of course stops at the gates of Paris and Versailles) to realise 'en combien de manières différentes l'homme peut être insupportable' (ibid.).

---

[1] Op. cit., p. 185.
[2] Julien Benda's views on the decline of French literature after classicism are a leitmotif of his literary criticism.

As a matter of fact, civilisation is on trial throughout the book and the trial ends without a verdict, for La Bruyère is in turn the judge, the witness for the prosecution, the lawyer for the defence, and the indignant or amused spectator.

Perhaps a study of the *Caractères* is also bound to end without a very definite conclusion. Some general features of the work seem, however, to emerge rather clearly. We see what has happened to that sphere which was the moralist's world, firmly centred on the universal aspects of human nature and tightly closed within accepted limitations. Not only does La Bruyère's imagination play on what was the outer surface of the sphere – the concrete, the short-lived, the brittle layer of civilisation – but so many of his preoccupations are off-centre and the pressure of his versatile concerns is so strong that the inner lining of the sphere cannot resist, and bursts. Remarks shoot outwards in all sorts of directions. His religious faith carries him into the fields of theology and philosophy, beyond the world of nature and reason; his sensibility beyond the comic vision into passionate satire. His moral purpose oversteps the boundaries which restricted the moralist's conception of *instruire* and he yields to the temptation of moralising.

Undoubtedly much of the book is devoted to a study of human nature. But the orthodox moralist concentrated on the most stable, however varied, characteristics of man, and, somewhat like a scientist, tried to establish laws explaining man's reactions and personality. Even exceptional cases were, with La Rochefoucauld, no more than an extension of well-acknowledged traits. La Bruyère at times, moved by idealistic yearnings, reaches out towards a world where genuine virtue is to be found and where we meet superior men who can no longer be said to fit into the pattern of humanity because they transcend all limitations.

The moralist knew very well how difficult it was to define a man's personality, how incoherent human reactions could appear. But it is highly indicative of La Bruyère's tendency to shift from the general to the particular that he should have been musing with a great deal of intellectual curiosity on freakish specimens of humanity, on somebody like Théodas, for instance, who

dit ridiculement des choses vraies, et follement des choses sensées et raisonnables... ('Des Jugements', 56)

a man, in fact, with a split personality:

...ce sont en lui comme deux âmes qui ne se connaissent point, qui ne dépendent point l'une de l'autre, qui ont chacune leur tour, ou leurs fonctions toutes séparées. (Ibid.)

or on a man like Straton whose individual features are so strange and contradictory that he will remain for ever an enigma:

Straton est né sous deux étoiles; malheureux, heureux dans le même degré. Sa vie est un roman: non, il lui manque le vraisemblable... ('De la Cour', 96)

A striking beginning, especially with the brusque movement of negation refuting the previous assumption. The end of the portrait is even more telling:

Le joli, l'aimable, le rare, le merveilleux, l'héroïque ont été employés à son éloge; et tout le contraire a servi depuis pour le ravaler: caractère équivoque, mêlé, enveloppé; une énigme; une question presque indécise.

The character thus described eludes any conclusion formulated in a complete and harmonious sentence. Note the staccato rhythm of the last clauses, the omission of verbs, and the way the fragmentation of the portrait is accentuated by the enumeration and juxtaposition of qualifying words.

These lines are perhaps La Bruyère's boldest experiment as a stylist; this is the point at which the style itself of the 'eccentric' moralist becomes a '*style éclaté*'.

All things considered, is not La Bruyère's literary personality as elusive as the individuality of his Straton, when we think of all the contradictions in the judgements he advances, his changing moods, the way he constantly shifts from one angle of vision to another, from the timeless to the ephemeral, from the panoramic picture of the court to the calyx of a tulip?

Yet if I dared venture a conclusion I would end with praise of some facets of the mind revealed by the *Caractères*: a fine sensibility, the imagination of a poet, the unusual suppleness of an intelligence stimulated by anything which comes its way and which finds several answers to one question, which moves with ease from the general to the particular, from the abstract to the concrete, from a sense of fitting dignity to the aesthetic attractions of elegance and wit – in short, taking the word in its most laudatory connotation, the mind of an extremely *civilised* man.

'THE PROPER STUDY OF MANKIND'

Any critical appreciation of works like La Rochefoucauld's *Maximes* or La Bruyère's *Caractères* inevitably leads to further thoughts on the particular attitude to life which the term 'moralist' implies.

We may be tempted to view it strictly in a historical perspective as representative of a given stage in the evolution of European thought since the Renaissance. We can see how, and to a certain extent why, the sixteenth-century ambitious humanist who wished to organise the whole cosmos round man, and his successor in the early seventeenth century who wanted to take all knowledge to be his province became the more sober moralist whose study, even more firmly based on the central position of man in the universe, explored only a severely restricted field. As such the moralist belongs to the second half of the seventeenth century, to the extent that the expression 'moralistes classiques', sometimes used in connection with La Rochefoucauld or La Bruyère, appears tautological.

Yet, although French classicism represents the golden age of the moralists, the use of the term is not limited to a seventeenth-century context. Is it because the moralist was concerned with the universal and permanent features of man that his attitude was able, for ever, to keep its relevance? His resilience, his power to survive, are perhaps easier to account for when we consider not so much what he is as what he is not. Although deeply committed to a search for the essential components of human nature, he is not a philosopher. His views are not attached to any of those fragile philosophical constructions which go on superseding one another and can even be altogether wiped out by a positivist outlook. Although he is interested in moral issues, since they are an integral part of man's social behaviour, he is not concerned to reform humanity and can distance himself from the ethics of a given society, relieved of the immediate task of edifying his readers. Although he is an observer of man and society, as impartial and as accurate as possible, we would hesitate to call him a sociologist or a psychologist in the modern sense of the word. He is not a scientist. His approach to his field of study does not rely on a specific method, does not depend on a technical training, does not require the use of a special language. His tool is that human reason which the reader will instinctively recognise as belonging to himself as well, that faculty of distinguishing between truth and falsehood, the cartesian *bon sens* which is supposed to be 'la chose du monde la mieux partagée'.

It is undeniable that the moralist holds a very secure place in the French tradition. The characteristic universality of his views suggests that they cut across the barriers of nationality; after all it was an English poet who stated that 'the proper study of mankind is man'. It is France, however, which has preserved and cherished the concept of what a moralist stands for. His presence is immediately acknowledged and welcomed whenever it is felt in works of literature even when very different from those of the classicist:

Il n'y a point d'unité complète dans l'homme, et presque jamais personne n'est tout à fait sincère ni tout à fait de mauvaise foi.

Here speaks the moralist in Benjamin Constant's *Adolphe*, as he speaks more than once elsewhere with the voice of Proust, of Valéry and of many others. And perhaps some French readers are the more receptive to the voice as at times the value-judgements of the moralist happen to coincide with their own lucid and pessimistic view of the human condition.

I have referred to the attitude of the moralist as a concept: we may well ask ourselves whether this 'ideal' model ever corresponds entirely to any known moralist. Although the basic features I have stressed were certainly present in the works of La Rochefoucauld and La Bruyère, they assume a somewhat different significance when we consider the complexity of the writers' views. We saw that La Bruyère did not accept the limitations which the moralist sets to his study of man and society. We might of course think of him as an exceptional case. But this would also be true, though to a lesser extent, of any moralist: his attitude is undoubtedly endowed with a particular resilience; it is also very precarious, for he is besieged with difficulties of all sorts. He cannot in fact avoid the pressure exerted by philosophical systems, nor the religious interpretations of human behaviour which mould the thoughts of his contemporaries, nor the ethical values set by the society in which he lives.[1] He cannot by his very position oppose the pressure of a system with a new system of his own, of accepted ethics with a new code of moral values; nor does he wish to do so, as he considers himself part of that society which he observes. Moreover his freedom from any acknowledged method of approach to the object of his study means that it is only in himself that he will find guiding lines for his explorations and their direction will be strongly influenced by his personality.

Hence the tension we perceive in the writings of La Rochefoucauld and La Bruyère between their ultimate aim as moralists – an impartial assessment of the human condition – and the pressures they are submitted to from the social reality around them and from within themselves as well. La Rochefoucauld's views on ethics are marked by that tension between orthodox morality and his own criteria of moral value, between his search for truth and his acceptance of social life. There is tension even in the language itself. We remember how loaded with theological implication the word *amour-propre* was, or how the moral connotations of a word – *paresse* for instance – persisted even when the term was used to define a psychological state which might be morally neutral. In La Bruyère also the tension is only too obvious. That he remained faithful to his position as a moralist is what Jules Brody has argued

---

[1] See Jules Brody's interesting remarks on the cartesian side of the *Caractères* in his article 'Images de l'homme chez La Bruyère' in *L'Esprit Créateur*, vol. xv, Spring–Summer 1975, pp. 68–78, and also for the philosophical and religious background to La Rochefoucauld's *Maximes* A. T. Levi's study of the French moralists which I mentioned in Chapter 1, p. 5.

very convincingly in stating that the picture of society we find in the *Caractères* is there to prove that everything described is no more than the momentary trappings hiding the essential nature of man.[1] That is quite true, but it is equally true that La Bruyère was fascinated by the society he condemned. As for the constant pull in him between his sensibility and his moral judgement, between the student of human nature and the 'moralisateur', it has been illustrated more than once in the preceding chapters.

It is perhaps this very tension which makes the reading of the *Maximes* and the *Caractères* such an enriching experience, even if we are faced with contradictions and ambiguities. This is also what gives such a strong individuality to each of the two works. One may occasionally indulge in a comparison bearing on a specific point, but the traditional sustained parallel between the two moralists is of little interest.

Most important of all, we should not forget that they were writers, artists in words. We are unlikely to overlook the writer as artist when we think of other authors like Molière or Madame de Lafayette or Racine, whose implicit attitude was also that of the moralist, because in their case we automatically think of the technical problems of a genre such as a play or a novel. In La Rochefoucauld and La Bruyère the attitude is explicit but the artistic achievement is there also and, as we have seen, raises questions concerning the literary language of the age.

We may wonder whether at times the art of the two moralists is not inseparable from the tension I have mentioned. It seems at its finest when the writers express a contradiction they cannot resolve between heart and reason:

S'il y a un amour pur et exempt du mélange de nos autres passions, c'est celui qui est caché au fond du cœur, et que nous ignorons nous-mêmes. (Maxim 69)

or when they deal with a paradox which reflects the complexity of the relations between art and nature:

[1] Op. cit., pp. 78–80.

Combien d'art pour rentrer dans la nature! combien de temps, de règles, d'attention et de travail pour danser avec la même liberté et la même grâce que l'on sait marcher; pour chanter comme on parle; parler et s'exprimer comme l'on pense;... ('Des Jugements', 34)

the sentence itself being a perfect exemplification of carefully achieved naturalness.

SELECT BIBLIOGRAPHY

A. MODERN EDITIONS

LA ROCHEFOUCAULD

Oeuvres de La Rochefoucauld, ed. D.-L. Gilbert et J. Gourdault, collection des 'Grands Ecrivains de la France', Paris, Hachette, 1868–83.

Oeuvres Complètes, ed. Martin Chauffier et Jean Marchand, 'Bibliothèque de la Pléiade', Paris, Gallimard, 1950.

Maximes et Réflexions, ed. Roland Barthes, 'Le Club français du Livre', Paris, 1961.

Maximes et Mémoires, J. Starobinski, 'Le monde en 10/18', Paris, 1964.

Réflexions ou Sentences et Maximes Morales, Réflexions Diverses, Dominique Secretan, 'Textes Littéraires Français', Geneva, Droz, 1967.

Maximes Suivies des Réflexions diverses, du Portrait de la Rochefoucauld par lui-même et des Remarques de Christine de Suède sur les Maximes, Jacques Truchet, Paris, Garnier, 1967.

La Justification de l'Amour, texte présenté par J. D. Hubert, Paris, Nizet, 1971.

LA BRUYÈRE

Oeuvres, G. Servois, collection des 'Grands Ecrivains de la France', Paris, Hachette, 1865–82.

Oeuvres Complètes, Julien Benda, 'Bibliothèque de la Pléiade', Paris, Gallimard, 1951.

Les Caractères de Théophraste traduits du grec avec les Caractères ou les Mœurs de ce siècle, Robert Garapon, Paris, Garnier, 1962.

Les Caractères, précédé de 'La Bruyère, du Mythe à l'Ecriture', Roland Barthes, 'Le monde en 10/18', Paris, 1963.

B. CRITICISM

(Most of the editions mentioned above contain important introductions to the works.)

Julien Benda, 'La Bruyère', in *Tableau de la Littérature Française, XVIIe–XVIIIe siècles*, Paris, Gallimard, 1939.

P. Bénichou, *Morales du Grand Siècle*, Paris, Gallimard, 1948.

'L'intention des "Maximes"' in *L'Ecrivain et ses travaux*, Corti, Paris, 1967.

Jules Brody, 'Sur le style de La Bruyère', in *L'Esprit Créateur*, Vol. XI, No. 2, Summer, 1971.

'Images de l'homme chez La Bruyère', in *L'Esprit Créateur*, Vol. XV, Nos. 1–2, Spring–Summer, 1975.

Amelia Bruzzi, *La Formazione delle 'Maximes' di La Rochefoucauld attraverso le edizioni originali*, Bologna, 1968.

J. Culler, 'Paradox and the language of morals in La Rochefoucauld', in *Modern Language Review*, January, 1973.

M. Guggenheim, 'L'homme sous le regard d'autrui ou le monde de La Bruyère', in P.M.L.A., LXXXI, No. 7, December, 1960.

Erica Harth, 'Classical Disproportion: La Bruyère's *Caractères*' in *L'Esprit Créateur*, Vol. XV, Nos. 1–2, Spring–Summer, 1975.

Louis Hippeau, *Essai sur la Morale de La Rochefoucauld*, Paris, Nizet, 1967.

E. D. James, 'Scepticism and positive values in La Rochefoucauld', in *French Studies*, October, 1969.

Michael S. Koppish, 'The Ambiguity of Social Status in La Bruyère's *Caractères*', in *L'Esprit Créateur*, Vol. XV, Nos. 1–2, Spring–Summer, 1975.

A. J. Krailsheimer, *Studies in Self-Interest from Descartes to La Bruyère*, Oxford, Clarendon Press, 1962.

J. de Lacretelle, 'La Rochefoucauld', in *Tableau de la Littérature Française, XIIe–XVIIIe siècles*, Paris, Gallimard, 1939.

Anthony Levi, *French Moralists*, Oxford, Clarendon Press, 1964.

W. G. Moore, 'La Rochefoucauld: une nouvelle anthropologie', in *Revue des Sciences Humaines*, October–December, 1953.

'The World of La Rochefoucauld's *Maximes*', in *French Studies*, October 1953.

French Classical Literature, Oxford, Clarendon Press, 1969.

La Rochefoucauld, his Mind and Art, Oxford, Clarendon Press, 1969.

P. Richard, *La Bruyère et ses 'Caractères'*, Amiens, Malfère, 1946.

C. Rosso, 'La Bruyère e la morale dei 'Caratteri', in *Filosofia*, April, 1964.

'Démarches et structures de compensation dans les *Maximes* de La Rochefoucauld', in *Bulletin de l'Association Internationale des Etudes Françaises*, No. 18, March, 1966.

La 'Maxime'. Saggi per une tipologia critica, Naples, Edizioni Scientifiche Italiane, 1968.

J. Starobinski, 'Complexité de La Rochefoucauld', in *Preuves*, May 1962.

'La Rochefoucauld et les Morales substitutives', in *Nouvelle Revue Française*, July 1966.

André Stegman, *Les Caractères de La Bruyère, bible de l'honnête homme*, collection 'Thèmes et Textes', Paris, Larousse, 1972.

L. Van Delft, *La Bruyère moraliste*, Geneva, Droz, 1971.

M. F. Zeller, *New Aspects of the Style in the Maxims of La Rochefoucauld*, Catholic University of America, vol. 48, Washington, D.C., 1954.

INDEX OF NAMES